DISCOVERING THE WRITER WITHIN

40 Days to More Imaginative Writing

Bruce Ballenger & Barry Lane

 Cincinnati, Ohio

For Leonard and Lillian Lane,
and for Karen.

Discovering the Writer Within: 40 Days to More Imaginative Writing. Copyright © 1989 by Bruce Ballenger and Barry Lane. Printed and bound in the United States of America. All rights reserved. No part of this book may be reproduced in any form or by any electronic or mechanical means including information storage and retrieval systems without permission in writing from the publisher, except by a reviewer, who may quote brief passages in a review. Published by Writer's Digest Books, an imprint of F&W Publications, Inc., 1507 Dana Ave., Cincinnati, Ohio 45207. First edition.

95 94 93   7 6 5

Library of Congress Cataloging-in-Publication Data

Ballenger, Bruce P.
    Discovering the writer within: 40 days to more imaginative writing/Bruce Ballenger & Barry Lane.
        p.   cm.
    Includes index.
    ISBN 0-89879-369-6
    1. Authorship. I. Lane, Barry. II. Title.
PN145.B424   1989   89-9046
808'.02—dc20   CIP

Acknowledgments

Though the act of writing is solitary work, writers do not work alone. We were both fortunate to be influenced by Donald Murray while teaching at the University of New Hampshire. His faith in the power of words to find their own way to meaning underpins this book. Peter Elbow, another pioneer in the teaching of writing, coined the expression "freewriting" years ago. We borrowed the term and incorporated several of his ideas. Others whose work broke ground before us include Natalie Goldberg, Gabrielle Lusser Rico, and William Zinsser. Goldberg's *Writing Down the Bones* helped us to believe that a book like ours would find readers, and Rico's *Writing the Natural Way* helped us to see the value of "clustering," a technique we espouse here. Zinsser's *On Writing Well,* a classic on nonfiction writing, contributed directly to sections of this book on humor and editing.

Susan Wheeler, a colleague at the University of New Hampshire, invented the exercise on Day Twelve and inspired us throughout the project. Brock Dethier's ideas — another master teacher and writer — also lurk behind many of the exercises here.

Other writing teachers who also influenced this work include Robert Connors, Carolyn Foley, Lester Fisher, Charles Gray, Gary Lindberg, Andrew Merton, Thomas Newkirk, Ted Walker, Thomas Williams, Mark Smith, and John Yount. We are grateful to them all.

Writer friends Charles Boyer, Rebecca Rule, Virginia Stuart, Alice Fogel, Richard Kraweic, Jane Harrigan, Roland Goodbody, Gerald Duffy, Sue Hertz, John Corra and Leaf Seligman helped with ideas and comments, some of which are included in the text.

Writing students Lorraine Kimball, Stephen Lewis, Christine Ruffner, and Kristine Doran inspired exercises and are directly or indirectly referred to in the text. Thank you for sharing your work with us.

Renee, Nick, Matt, and Miles Bodimeade helped with artistic inspiration and illustrations for the Grammar Police and the Horse Race of Meaning. We are particularly indebted to Jean Fredette of Writer's Digest Books, whose enthusiasm and support for this idea helped bring it to print.

Many people helped us to survive while writing this book. Thanks to Bob Eger and Karen McCarthy; Marilyn, Richard, and Julie Anne Worth for help with titles and Vermont winters; Leslie, Stephen, and Abigail Goodrich for being there when we needed them most; Raymond Young for keeping the woodpile high when spirits were low.

Finally, this book could not have been written without the love, partnership, and ruthless editing of Carol-Lee Lane, and the constant joy and inspiration of Jessie Lynn. Carmelita Pope Wood unwittingly supplied material for parts of this book and helped one of its authors understand that risk and discipline are parents to most creative work. He has not forgotten.

Contents

Workouts for Writing Problems

I've got a bad case of writer's block . . . Days 1, 2, 3, 14, 38

I'm feeling really discouraged . . . Days 14, 38

I have a hard time getting started writing . . . Days 2, 3

I have a hard time with beginnings . . . Day 15

I have a hard time with endings . . . Day 39

I never revise . . . Days 8, 16

I'm ready to revise, but I don't know how to begin . . . Days 13, 17-19, 32, 34

I want to find readers who will help me . . . Day 33

I can't find anything to write about . . . Days 1-7

I've got too much to write about and need to focus . . . Days 11, 13, 15, 17-19, 36

I need to improve my ear for dialogue . . . Days 24, 25, 27

I want to become more observant . . . Days 8, 9, 11, 16, 26, 37

I have problems with interviews . . . Days 24, 26

I hate using the library for research . . . Day 28

I want to write humor, but I'm not very funny . . . Days 22, 23

My writing doesn't have enough detail . . . Days 5, 8, 9, 12, 36

My writing sounds boring . . . Days 20, 21, 32

I am terrified of making grammatical mistakes . . . Days 2, 32

I don't know what point-of-view to choose for my short story . . . Day 35

I have trouble being imaginative . . . Days 29-31

I don't know whether I'm making progress . . . Days 38, 40

Introduction

You have always thought you could be a writer. It is a feeling you have, a little voice in the back of your head whispering, "Someday I'm gonna write a book about this." You wait. You haunt stationery stores looking for the right size pad, the right spiral-bound notebook, the right pen or pencil. You scribble ideas for romance novels and thrillers; you write the first sentence of your autobiography one hundred times. You keep a journal. You buy a typewriter, computer, a box of number two pencils. You dream of going to Paris and sitting in cafes. You drink a lot of strong coffee.

Books tell you how to become rich and famous, how to get an agent, how to field your first movie sale. They are written by famous authors who are willing to share a few tips. You wouldn't mind being rich and famous, but what you really want to do is translate this feeling in your guts into words. You don't care about North American serial rights; you care about what you have to say.

Most of your teachers didn't help you. Your essays were battlefields of red ink, you wrote run-on sentences, your participles dangled. You didn't use all of the weekly vocabulary words. You worked for *A*'s to please them but you never really cared what you did on your summer vacation and you never wrote about the confusion you felt at your grandmother's funeral or the anger over your parents' divorce, or about how the mailman, Mr. Topham, used to say "Nice day," but he never smiled or even stopped frowning at the children in the neighborhood.

Maybe you dropped out of high school. Maybe you finished college or graduate school or technical school. You became a plumber, a homemaker, a doctor, a waiter, a parent, a singer, a lawyer, a nun, a sax player, a senator, a nurse, a truck driver. You have dreams and fantasies which haunt and delight you. You want to discover the universe inside you. You've written a few stories, essays, and poems, and maybe even had some luck publishing. But the book of your life has grown to James Michener-like proportions. It's full of diners and dragons, truck stops and extraterrestrials. You want to begin writing it, but you don't know how to begin or where to begin or what to begin. All you know is that little voice saying you must write and late at night as you lie in bed trying to sleep, a typewriter taps away in the dark closet of your mind. There's a writer in there. If only you could open the door.

We wrote this book for you. We have taught writing for years and know that the only way to become a writer is through writing. This book is not like any other you will read because you will write more than half of it. You will sit down for thirty minutes a day and write. You will learn your unique writing process, helpful ways to generate ideas and information, techniques to help develop and shape your material, new avenues to explore in your dreams and memories. And most of all you will learn the power of writing as a tool for seeing yourself and the world around you.

Everyone will use this book differently. There is no recipe for good writing, only constant trial and error and discovery. Most of us were taught wrong in grade school. We were taught that writing was grammar and vocabulary and five-paragraph themes with introductions, bodies, and conclusions. This book will teach you that writing is ideas, sounds, smells, feelings, dreams, people, places, fantasies. Writing is that mole on your father's left earlobe that you always stared at when he held you in his lap. It's that diesel fuel smell that reminds you of your grandmother's cellar where you played army, watched her haul the sheets out of the washing machine, and watched her try to cough out the emphysema in her lungs. Writing is that dream you once had about being cast as Judas in *Jesus Christ Superstar,* or the crazy ideas you used to get while driving in your car, ideas about how the world would be if elephants ran the stock market or sparrows formed a passenger airline for ants. Writing is fun. Writing is hard work. Writing is ———————————————.

Get a notebook of some kind. Make it something you feel comfortable carrying around with you. Small spiral-bounds are nice, or maybe you like the black and white composition books or loose-leaf folders. Haunt a stationery store. Breathe deep the smell of pencil and fresh cut paper. This is a writer's heaven. Find a pen—a Flair or rollerball or ballpoint. Get different colors for each day of the week, or buy pencils with different leads. Indulge yourself. You are going to write.

Set aside thirty minutes a day. It could be before work in the morning or late at night when the dishes are done and the children are in bed. Find a place to sit in the house or on the porch, in the garage, or at Burger King. It should be a comfortable place, but not too comfortable. You don't want to fall asleep. Make sure there is a clock or watch nearby you can use to time yourself. Know the value of writing while sipping tea or coffee. Stay away from alcohol and drugs. The world has enough tortured geniuses. Stay healthy.

You are ready to begin, but before you do, there are a few things you should know.

1) You can't make a mistake when you use this book. If it seems after reading the Writer to Writer section on the day's exercise, that you've done the work differently, congratulations. You are an original thinker. It's people like you who have helped these exercises to evolve into their present state. Drop us a line and tell us what you did. We'll give you an acknowledgment in the sequel to *Discovering the Writer Within*.

2) This book is written by two writers, one fiction and one nonfiction. Because we are very different writers we decided to keep both our voices in the book. We also believe that our individual struggles as writers in different genres will help you to compare the processes required for each genre. Each Writer to Writer section is initialed by either Barry or Bruce. By the end of the book you'll probably be able to tell us apart by our voices (especially if we start to argue).

3) Though the book is designed consecutively as forty days of writing workouts, it doesn't have to be used that way. Consult "Workouts for Writing Problems" (page x) and do the exercises for the days that correspond to what you need to learn. Or, if on any particular day it stops being fun, skip to another day or go back and work some more on material which inspired you earlier. You are the teacher and the student. You know when you're learning.

Forty days is the period of time most mental institutions hold patients before committing them. When you're through writing this book, you can decide whether you want a a room at the Writer's Hotel, or whether you want to wander penless through the world. Whatever you decide, you will have learned something.

At this point we should say something inspiring or quote a famous writer in a way that sends you rushing to your desk. But we will resist the temptation, so that you can simply turn the page and start learning what it is *you* have to say.

Day One:
Hunting Is Not Those Heads
on the Wall

Begin writing, starting with the four words below. Write quickly, without thinking too much about what you want to say before you write it. Write for ten minutes. Time yourself.

When I write, I . . .

Seeing What You Said

What attitude toward writing did you take? Were you extremely critical about your writing, or did you express enthusiasm about it? Was it hard to write fast for ten minutes? Did you run out of things to say?

Read over what you wrote. Underline sentences, passages, or phrases that strike you as particularly important or interesting, for whatever reason.

Writer to Writer

Some of you might want to be writers or might simply love to write, doing it not only without complaint but for the sheer pleasure of hearing yourself on the page. Maybe you've always felt that way. Maybe you've spent Saturday afternoons composing stories and writing them down and reading them to your best friend. Maybe you've faithfully kept a journal for years. Maybe you got A's in English, and maybe you even liked *The Scarlet Letter*.

A few years back, I would have hated you for being like that. I envied people who made writing seem so easy and fun, because it was just the opposite for me. As a child, I composed stories in my head—that's something we all do when we're young—but I didn't like to write them down. To write them down was to put them to death. For years, I tried to keep a journal, but the entries quickly grew shorter and shorter and finally dwindled to nothing. I hated high school English and high school English hated me. I clung to my *C*'s for dear life.

In short, writing was a painfully slow process for me and remained so for many years. I recalled that pain when I first did this exercise. I wrote about my obsession with neat drafts and IBM selectric typewriters, and how I'd wanted to write beautiful prose right out of the gate. I wrote about the white, glaring, pupilless eyes of a blank page, daring me to write the first word.

Several years ago, I read an essay by the writer, Amiri Baraka, titled "Hunting Is Not Those Heads on the Wall." I return to the piece time and again as I struggle to write and to teach writing. Baraka argues that how we bring art into being is far more important than the thing itself. The painting, the poem, the article, or the story—the "artifacts" that remain after the artist has completed the act of creation—are only "shadowy replicas" of the thought that made them.

"Thought is more important than art," he writes. "Art is one of the many products of thought. An impressive one, perhaps the most impressive one, but to revere art, and have no understanding of the process that forces it into existence, is finally not even to understand what art is."

The truth of Baraka's words became clear to me one night while talking to a good friend about our families. We were talking in the loose and unstructured way that friends do (contrary to the way I used to write), and I realized that after an hour of this, we had both stumbled on significant insights about her relationship with her father and mine with my mother. We had not *tried* to be insightful, but we had unwittingly created the conditions that made it possible. We had no preconceived notions about the outcome of our conversation. Rather, we were willing to say things that were not completely figured out, and shared delight in the *act* of talking frankly to each other.

Not long after that I began to pay more attention to the way I go about writing and less to what I want to turn out—to the process rather than the artifact. I realized that if my writing could be as free and easy as that conversation with my friend, *it* would yield more insight and surprise, too. And it could be rewarding, rather than slow and painful.

Beginning with the four words "When I Write, I . . ." may have started you thinking about your writing process. Maybe your journal entry was a celebration of a lifetime of writing poems on the backs of telephone bills, or more like mine: a long scribbled sigh about how hard it is sometimes.

Whether you find writing a constant joy or a constant struggle, it is useful to see yourself as two writers instead of one—a critic and a child—who must learn to get along but often don't. Even though you love writing, you are apt to hear the loud voice of your internal critic—your "Watcher at the Gates," as novelist Gail Godwin calls it — always daring you to fail. In many of the exercises that follow, we'll ask you to silence that Watcher to give the child a chance to dream, to imagine, to surprise you with what it knows, transforming the blank page from an adversary into a playground of possibility.

BB

Follow Through

All writers have Watchers that will sometimes try to close the doors of inspiration. Mine is finicky about liking Pentel pens, and constantly reminds me that my father was a better writer than I'll ever be. It insists that I write only in the morning, and that I will never learn how to write poetry. It would rather I didn't write fast because the writing is too messy and incoherent. It whispers words I'll never learn how to spell.

One way to stop your Watcher from carping at you, making it difficult to get any work done, is to write your Watcher a letter. Sound off. Get it off your chest. Point out to your internal critic what it says that helps and what doesn't. Write quickly for five minutes:

Dear Watcher,

Day Two:
Look at the Flowers

Think of childhood experiences that left lasting impressions on you, either positive or negative. List five or ten and pick the one that wants to be written about. Set aside ten minutes to sit down somewhere and "freewrite" about the experience.

Keep in mind the following principles of freewriting.

1) Write quickly, without thinking about what you want to say before you say it. Keep your pen moving.

2) Don't censor yourself. Resist the temptation to "fix" sentences that have grammatical problems, or that seem awkward and unclear. If you write something that sounds stupid, don't worry about it.

3) Don't worry about coherence. If you feel like wandering off on a tangent, do it. If you stall out on a line of thinking, skip a line and move on to another idea or memory. Just keep writing.

4) Relax and have fun. Let the memories flood back, and capture what you can on the page.

Now begin freewriting about your experience. Let your memories fill the page. Start anywhere. Ready? Begin.

Seeing What You Said

Read over your freewrite. Mark lines or passages that surprise you or that are particularly interesting, for whatever reason.

Were you surprised at how much you remembered?

Did you experience a kind of exhilarating rush as the writing ran out ahead of you? Or did you find that you were bothered at the sloppiness of the writing?

Did you love the freedom of free association, or did you feel guilty every time you drifted off on a tangent? Did you give yourself permission to write nonsense, or did the "bad" writing drain your confidence?

Writer to Writer

One morning when I was two years old, I crawled out of my bed and scribbled flowers with purple crayon on the white walls. They were sloppy flowers with great looping petals and long stems that curled onto the wooden floor.

"Look at the flowers!" I yelled to my mother, who was dusting in the hallway. She took two steps into the room and shouted, "What are you doing? My clean white walls! Get out!"

There are two voices that speak to me as I write. One is intuitive, unruly, and wild; the other is rational, controlled, and judgmental. One falls in love with ideas, makes astonishing discoveries, and dreams on like a madman shouting, "Move over, Tolstoy, here I come!" The other is contained and critical, eyeing the page from a distance and sneering at misspelled words and ungrammatical sentences. "You can do better than that, I hope," it says. One voice says, "Look at the flowers I'm making!" The other, "Look at the mess you've made!"

Like Bruce, when I first began writing, I thought it was miserable work. I had learned that from a series of English teachers who still parade through my mind in a cloud of red ink and mimeo fluid. They convinced me that you had to choose the right word, you had to have a large vocabulary, your introduction had to mirror your conclusion, and above all, you had to be profound. I remember essays and stories coming back to me scarred with the red pen and pithy comments in the margin like "awk," "run on," "word choice," "cliché." I was a poor speller, I couldn't write a grammatical sentence if my life depended on it, and nothing I said was original. Nobody ever told me that F. Scott Fitzgerald and Evelyn Waugh were terrible spellers or that Ernest Hemingway's first drafts were chock-a-block full of run-on sentences and dangling participles. Nobody ever asked me the one question that would have made sense: "What are you trying to say?"

It took me years of struggling with my internal critic before I could sit down in front of a blank sheet of paper without a dictionary or a thesaurus, or hold a pen without thinking first about the metaphors or similes I should plug into a poem or essay. I am not alone. As Bruce mentioned, we all have a "Watcher at the Gates" who stands there scrutinizing the fruit of our imagination. To begin writing, it is necessary to excuse the Watcher. Get your critic out of the room so your imagination can do its playful work without being hammered with discouraging thoughts. Only later in the writing process, when distance and critical judgment are needed, will your Watcher be a helpful ally.

Think of your imagination as a big, freshly plowed, fertile field. Your critic is a gardener with only a pair of grass clippers and a few thoughts on how the plants should look. You are the sun, the rain, and the seeds of ideas growing beneath in darkness. The plants will all grow in their own directions if you let them. You mustn't let the gardener snip off the green sprouts before the sunlight touches them, or trim a rose so it will look like a cabbage plant. You must feel the excitement of letting them grow, chanting always to yourself, "Look at the flowers I'm making!"

BL

Follow Through

Without looking back at your first attempt, freewrite for another ten minutes about the same experience. If your Watcher intrudes, write faster and more wildly—let your pen, spiraling over the page, push the critic out the door. Don't write words. Write thoughts. Don't write sentences. Write smells, sights, sounds, ideas. . . .

During my first year teaching at the University of New Hampshire, a professor cornered me and said, "Barry, you have to be really careful about what you put in people's mailboxes. The memo you passed out for the writer's series had typos and spelling mistakes and grammatical errors. You have to remember there are full professors reading this stuff." He was right. I had been a little careless. But why did I feel so totally devastated, like some terrible secret was finally out? Why did I slink back to my office like a wanted criminal? I told my feelings to Gerry Duffy, a fellow grad student, who replied, "Oh, Grammar Police got you, eh?" That night I wrote this comic piece. I read it to my students, so they know to bolt their doors while writing first drafts.

Grammarnoia

The story you are about to read is true. Only the grammar and punctuation have been changed to protect the innocent.

He was in his office late at night. He was writing. There were three loud raps on the door. He scratched out sentences. He hid paper under the file cabinet. He pulled the paper from his typewriter and stuffed it in his mouth.

The door exploded open and two men barged in. Both wore tweed sportcoats with wrinkled copies of Strunk and White in the breast pockets. They stood in a cloud of chalk dust, flailing their red Flairs.

"Grammar Police. Drop the pen!"

They flashed their IDs. Both full professors. Harvard '56, Columbia '64. They yanked the piece of yellow second copy from his mouth and ransacked the drawers.

"Run-ons," the older one said, scoring his pen over the wrinkled piece of paper.

"Comma splices," the other man said. "Gerunds everywhere."

They rolled the teacher away from the desk and faced him against the wall.

"But I take a process-oriented approach," the teacher said.

"Sure buddy, we've heard that before. Spell necessary."

"I'm not spelling anything till I see my lawyer."

"Punctuate this sentence." They shoved a piece of paper into his lap. "THE MAN WHO WAS HAPPY EATING WHEATIES LIKED OTHER CEREALS TOO."

"I'm not punctuating anything."

"How long have you been teaching at this university?"

"A year."

"Put it in a complete sentence."

"I have been teaching at this university a year."

"Put it in the pluperfect."

"I taught—"

"Book him."

"But this is only a first draft."

"Sure, buddy, and we're going on our first little ride downtown. Maybe you can have a little talk with the spelling squad, too. Spell necessary."

"It begins with N-E," he said.

"You hear that Joe? We've got a real Phi Beta Kappa on our hands here."

They laughed as they slid bits of crinkled paper into their manila envelopes.

"You can't do this. There's nothing wrong with being ungrammatical as long as you do it in the privacy of your own room with a consenting piece of paper."

They thumbed through their Strunk and Whites in unison.

"Listen to this, Meathead: 'There is no excuse for grammatical ambiguity.' "

"But what about content? What about subject? What about voice? What about me?"

They clamped two steel parentheses over his wrists.

"We'll deal with you, don't worry."

In the squad car on the way to the station they asked him how he could expect to teach college freshmen to write when he could barely punctuate a sentence himself. He was silent, his mind recalling all the spelling bees from which he was eliminated in the first round; his eyes peering through the gallons of red ink on every essay he had ever handed a teacher.

"I was a victim of an ungrammatical childhood," he told the judge. "My mother spoke in fragments. My father always hesitated in mid clause. In their eyes, I was parenthetical. I lived between the commas."

The judge wore a commencement robe and mortar board. Hanging from the tassles were dashes, semicolons, periods.

"Spell necessary," he said.

"Hopeless."

"No, necessary."

"Impossible."

"No, necessary."

He had looked up the word at least 3,000 times in his lifetime, and he still could not be sure if there were one *c* and two *s*'s or one *s* and two *c*'s.

He closed his eyes and imagined the firing squad—ten high school English teachers with horn-rimmed glasses and eraser-pink ears. His hooded body slumped meekly in the chair. *Long live meaning*, he would cry at the last moment, or, *Substance over form forever*.

"N-E-C-"

In his mind there were two *c*'s, but suddenly, at the very last moment, one of them floated away like a balloon into the stratosphere.

"E-S-S-A-R-Y. Necessary."

"Indeed, necessary," the judge said.

He was paroled the next morning and was last seen chasing run-ons through a parking lot in New Jersey.

Day Three:
Let the Rivers Rush

Spend a few moments thinking about the unforgettable places you've been. They can be close to home or far away, places you've been to recently or long ago.

Choose one. Now freewrite about it for ten full minutes. Start by transporting yourself back into the place and describe what you see, smell, feel, hear. Remember the rules of freewriting: Write quickly without stopping, and let the words run out ahead of you. Don't worry about the quality of the writing or where it's heading. If you find yourself writing about something other than the place you started with, don't worry. If you run out of things to say, write about having nothing to say. Just keep your pen moving for the full ten minutes.

Stretch your fingers. Ready? Begin writing.

Seeing What You Said

Is it getting easier to write fast without stopping?

Did you wander off on a tangent (perhaps to another place, or an event, or a person, or even about the exercise) that seemed even more interesting than what you started with?

Did you remember many specifics about the place that surprised you? Do you see any clues in the writing about why it is significant to you? Did the writing resurrect old feelings or uncover new feelings about the place? Have you changed the way you see the place since you were there last?

Read over what you wrote and underline or mark words, lines, or passages that strike you.

Writer to Writer

Like Barry, I hear two voices when I write. One is intuitive, full of feeling, ideas, and images that seem to be rushing with the speed and force of the Yellowstone River in May. This voice often makes wild connections between what I've seen and thought, and it surprises me by what it says. Though it sometimes speaks in a timid hush, this voice inside my head makes me want to write.

The other voice often speaks much more loudly to me when I have the pen in my hand. It is a critical voice, always on the lookout for error: the faulty logic, the lack of coherence, the misspelled word. At times my critical voice strangely takes on the sound of my eighth grade English teacher, Mrs. O'Neill. Like her, it has very high standards, constantly reminding me that writers are supposed to write well. *Always.* In its worst mood, this voice cruelly dares me to fail.

This brooding Watcher is uncomfortable with freewriting. It's the voice that, for some of you, whispered that this is a stupid exercise or a stupid book; or whined that you can never remember anything about the places you've been; or seduced you into stopping your freewrite after four minutes because you needed to eat an Almond Joy or were using the wrong pen. Our personal Watcher does not need to be our enemy. It must not be. We need our internal critic to help us make sense of the wonderful, but unruly, excesses of our imagination.

Those of you who were able to excuse your Watchers in this exercise, or the one yesterday about a childhood experience, may have experienced the rush of words that made the ten minutes fly by—words that revealed to you what you didn't know you knew. When I did this freewrite, I was drawn back into a canyon in Montana where, some years ago, I spent long summer days fishing for trout. I suddenly found myself writing about an abandoned railroad tunnel through which I had to walk to reach the lower portion of the stream. The tunnel was long and dark, and during the day, rattlesnakes would sometimes coil themselves along the rusty tracks, resting in the cool dampness. The writing reminded me of walking slowly through the tunnel, one step at a time, tapping the track ahead with the tip of my fly rod, alert to a sudden hiss and rattle.

It is a powerful image: that black tunnel bored through the pale stone of a mountain; the sound of my slowly shuffling feet; and the tap, tap of the fishing rod on gravel and rusting steel.

I didn't think of it before I wrote it down. I wrote it down first and then it surprised me. That's what happens when, through fast writing, I am able to excuse my Watcher and listen to my other voice.

There are many rivers running through our heads—the one that binds us with place is particularly deep and fast—and we need to let some of their waters flow to the blank page, unimpeded by the internal critic that demands that we always think *before* we write. Learn to think *through* writing. Let the rivers rush.

BB

Follow Through

In this exercise, you were asked to choose one unforgettable place you've been and freewrite about it. Place plays an important part in most of our lives, and it's an important source of material for writing. Finish today's writing by building a quick list in your journal of other places that might have significance to you. Choose another place from this list and freewrite about it for ten minutes.

Day Four:
The Thicker Stew

Take a few minutes and look over your list of places. Pause a moment in each place and listen for voices; look for people.

Make a new list of these people and add other people whom you've known and can't forget. Let your list grow quickly, spreading to different areas of your life.

Pick one person that jumps out at you and freewrite about him or her for ten minutes. Start anywhere, perhaps with his voice, or your first impression of her, or how your relationship has changed through the years. Anywhere. You are an artist doing a quick thumbnail sketch with words. Let your pen do the remembering.

Seeing What You Said

Read over what you've written and circle the places where your memories of the person surprised you. Underline the places where your pen went flat, where you seemed to be talking in circles.

Does the person come alive on the page for you? Or does your freewrite seem like a pale shadow of the image you were going for? Was the person easy to write about? Or did the words come slow and laboriously?

When you set the writing aside, what new things do you remember about the person? Do you want to write more about them, or is your pen already thinking of somebody else?

Writer to Writer

When I remember the old railroad bridge on Washington Street in Dover, New Hampshire, I immediately see my childhood friend Johnny Manning slouching over the rail in his faded dungaree jacket, launching a gob of spit into the algae-choked Cocheco River. When I think of the algae-choked Cocheco River, I see, years later, my buddies Bill Sturrock and Bob Eger sailing at low tide past the sewer plant in a little sky-blue boat. Bill sings "Santa Lucia" while Bob holds the tiller steady through the narrow channel.

When I think of Winterpark, Florida, I no sooner smell the sickly sweet scent of orange blossoms than I see Jimmy Dunkle in his blue bell-bottoms heading for the ABC lounge to buy three tiny bottles of vodka with the money his wife gave him for gas. The French alps are indelibly stained with the memory of Michel and Cheri, two down-and-out gypsies with whom I spent two days in a vacant youth hostel.

Bruce's workout on place made me remember all the people who inhabit those places. As a fiction writer, I often begin with a character, and places are colored by these characters. Once, on a solo trip to Walt Disney World in Florida, I started a conversation with an old woman who sat next to me on the bus. It turned out the woman was Jewish and from Warsaw. As we spoke, I noticed the number tattoo under her left forearm. She seemed lonely so I spent the day with her. Standing in line for the Skyway to Fantasyland with this woman made me think of all the other lines she had stood in during the war. I could see bizarre parallels between the mechanized fantasies of Disney World and the sinister death machines of the Nazi camps. Disney World was a new, much darker, place.

Years later I wrote a story about the woman, called "Survivors." The story is about a young Jewish man who meets a Holocaust survivor at Disney World. When I read the story now it feels incomplete. I think of all the facts about Eva Schwartz I didn't include—how her second husband owned a chain of supermarkets in Montreal, how she described her recent visit to Egypt, how she scoffed at my attempts to speak Yiddish saying, "You speak Jew like a goy."

Friedrich Nietzsche once tried to describe the inability of writing to capture it all. He said, "Think of all the great books ever written. Now close your eyes and think about one moment of real life."

His point is well taken. When we write, we can't include everything. We must focus on the information that's most important. The people we write about are not the same ones who walk around in real life. The cornstarch of imagination and memory flows through the pen and writing becomes a thicker stew.

Once I wrote a story about a jazz drummer who couldn't get his bass pedal to make the right sound. In real life I had lived with the man, but left before he could solve the problem. In the story, the drummer finally realizes it's the complacent rhythms of his life that won't let the sound come. He locks himself in his room and plays all night until the sound appears in the morning.

A year ago, I met the drummer in a bar in Portsmouth, New Hampshire. I told him about the story and asked him if he'd ever fixed his bass pedal. "Oh that," he said, shaking his head, "that was all physical."

I am not a prophet or clairvoyant, but I have an imagination and I have learned to trust it when I have my pen in hand. The people I write about live as much inside me as they do in the outside world. When I write about Mitch, the mailman I knew as a child, I also write about the pair of glinting eyes that peered through the metal slot in the front door and waited for the sound of his heavy boots on the wooden porch.

Writing is a thicker stew.

BL

Follow Through

As a fun project, reserve several pages in your journal and make a list of every person you've ever known. Find your own methods of remembering. You may want to work chronologically or simply catalog different areas of your life. Don't labor. Don't worry if you don't get everybody. Let your list grow in leaps and spurts. Carry it with you to work and muse about it in your spare time.

Later, go back over your list and circle any names that seem to jump out at you. Make brief notes about them or do ten minute freewrites. Keep them as a reservoir of ideas to draw on in the future.

Day Five:
A Roomful of Details

Imagine a room you spent a lot of time in as a child. It could be your bedroom, the family room in the old house, the bright kitchen where your grandmother kneaded dough with her strong hands. Transport yourself back into that room and "brainstorm" a quick but specific list of everything you see.

Brainstorming, like freewriting, has a few rules. It demands that you excuse your Watcher. Make a fast list (I find it often comes in waves) of whatever comes to mind. Don't censor yourself. Don't try to make sense. Don't try to write words or phrases that sound good. Much of your list may be "code words" that have meaning only for you and may be undecipherable to anyone else. Keep building your list, looking in every corner of the room in your memory until you can write no more. Set aside five minutes for this.

Ready? Begin.

Look over your list. Were you surprised at how much you remembered? Look for one detail on your list that triggers more memories, or seems strangely charged with meaning. Circle it, and, beginning with that object, launch into a seven-minute freewrite. Let the writing run out ahead of you. Don't think before you write. Just write and see where the words take you.

Ready? Start writing.

Seeing What You Said

Which did you find easier to do, brainstorming or freewriting?

Were you amazed at how much you remembered of that room from your childhood? Was there more than one detail on your list you wanted to write about?

Did the freewrite take you out of the room to someplace else? Did the exercise reveal anything to you about who you were as a child, or who you are now?

Was your writing rich with specifics or was it vague?

Writer to Writer

We are walking warehouses of experience. Stored away on the back shelves of our minds are the treasures of memory; in some cases, things we've forgotten are there. When I did this exercise, I imagined the bedroom where I spent fifteen years of my life. I remembered the deep red color of the burlap wallpaper, the green clay Buddha on my dresser, the white porcelain horse with the broken tail, the long crack in the window, my collection of yellow plastic 45 rpm records in the rickety cabinet. I also remembered a photograph of a ten-year-old awkwardly standing next to Ernie Banks, the legendary Chicago Cubs first baseman. That ten-year-old was me, and the shot was taken one July day at Wrigley Field before a game with the Los Angeles Dodgers.

I had forgotten about that picture, that moment, and that time in my life when going to a baseball game was like going to church. I couldn't wait to begin freewriting about it, and when I did, I could see the beginnings of what might be an essay about being the son of a Chicago television personality, and my own small yearnings for fame (see page 67). And it all began with a seemingly innocuous list of the objects in my bedroom.

Material and ideas for essays, poems, short stories, and articles will grow that way—like flowers on blank, barren walls, as Barry said a few days ago—but you must free your writing to make it possible. That's one purpose of the past four days' exercises. Hopefully you are finding it less difficult, maybe even easy, to think *through* writing rather than always thinking *before* you write. But it takes practice because most of us were not trained to write that way. We were taught that writing is only a vehicle for expressing what we already know, not a means of finding out what we didn't know we knew.

I had a teacher in high school who insisted that I make an outline before I wrote anything. It seemed like good advice. It's no wonder that my prose back then was dull to write and dull to read. I became so wedded to my tidy plans about what I should say and when I should say it that there was no room for surprise, no room to even change my mind.

I don't have anything against outlines, but I no longer want to impose them on my writing. I want to be more playful, freer to let the words tell me what I think. In the days that follow, we'll continue to propose exercises like this one that help you learn to write fast, and even to write badly. We'll continue to coax that imaginative voice out of hiding to tell you what you think and feel.

I am always on the lookout for what the poet Richard Hugo called the "triggering subjects"—things that suddenly allow me into those back rooms of my mind, launch me into writing, and lead me to things I want to explore more deeply. In this exercise, what triggered my writing was something quite specific: a black and white photograph over my dresser that I had forgotten about until it appeared on the page of my journal. That photograph was a starting point that propelled me toward the subject I discovered I really wanted to write about: growing up with a famous mother.

Writers are constantly on the lookout for significant details such as these. They often unlock the doors of that wonderful warehouse of material we carry around in our heads from which essays, poems, and stories are built.

BB

Follow Through

Choose another significant detail from your list above, and freewrite for another seven minutes, using the detail as a starting point. Or see if any of these things might trigger more writing. Brainstorm a list of:

- Your heroes
- Risks you've taken
- Toys you played with as a child
- Food you love to eat
- Pets that meant something to you
- Music that has touched you
- Books that influenced you
- Possessions you've treasured
- Embarrassing moments
- Teachers you've had
- Sexual experiences

Find something that begs to be written about. Freewrite for ten minutes, starting with that. Let the writing run out ahead of you. Rummage through the back shelves of your mind and discover all the treasures you've stored there.

Day Six:
Looking for the Lump in Your Throat

Look over your work for the last five days and search for subjects that are ripe with meaning, the kind of subjects that make you think, ''I could write about that, but where would I begin?'' It could be a person, a place, a detail from your room, or anything, as long as it's big and unwieldy.

Place the subject (the name of the place or person, the detail, the experience) in the middle of a blank page in your notebook and just stare at it for a minute. Close your eyes and let your mind hover and dive around it like a hummingbird circling around a bouquet of sticky flowers.

You're ready to begin clustering.

Draw a circle around your subject. This is the nucleus. Free associate branches of words fanning out from the center. As with freewriting and brainstorming, don't think before you write. Let the words come in waves. Don't be afraid if your words don't mean anything to anyone else but you. Let your pen do the thinking. When one strand runs out, go back to the nucleus and start another. When you come across a word in a branch that is too evocative to skip over, let that word be a nucleus to sprout another branch. If your mind goes blank, doodle, darkening lines or circles until a new branch sprouts. Let your words grow like ivy on a great elm over the clean page, so that when you're done it may look something like the one I did on the country Israel, which is pictured on the following page.

Seeing What You Said

When you look at your cluster are there any strands that seem particularly interesting or provocative, or does it seem like a big mess?

Do you see things that puzzle you and surprise you in some strands? Are there contradictions? Mixed feelings? Or did the words come out just as you expected them to? Was clustering a comfortable technique for you or did your Watcher keep telling you how silly it was?

Did you allow yourself to follow strands until they fizzled out or did you keep running back to the nucleus for more fuel? Did you discover new subjects to make the nucleus of a new cluster?

Are you dying to cluster about other things that aren't in your journal, such as your mother or the man who empties your trash, or was this a weird experiment that will never be as useful as freewriting or brainstorming?

Writer to Writer

It's easy to say that writing is not carpentry but gardening, that essays and stories grow on the page and are not manufactured in some grammar factory inside our heads. But the truth is, we have been taught the latter for years by well-meaning teachers and it's hard to stop our words from marching single file across the page. Though it might seem crazy at first, clustering is a wonderful way to chase down ideas without being slowed up by sentences and para-

graphs. Like yesterday's brainstorming, it allows a writer a chance to explore ideas without putting them into rigid form. Clustering can give you a little elbow room to play with an idea and discover the "triggering subjects" Bruce talked about yesterday.

I clustered about Israel, a country I've visited twice—in 1978 and in 1986. Both times it was a powerful and confusing experience for me, a young Jew who was not quite sure what it meant to be either young or Jewish.

As I worked the cluster, I realized how rich the subject was. I found myself remembering many things I'd forgotten. I remembered Jake Jennings, a congressman from Philadelphia who sat next to me on the Olympic airways jet from Athens. He and another congressman were on a fact-finding mission for President Carter. The other man insulted the stewardess, grabbing her by the shoulders and pointing to the Greek letters on her sweater, saying, "Remember Jake? The fraternity? Delta Chi." The stewardess scowled back at him. I remember watching a bomb squad dismantle a white Mercedes Benz in full view of a cafe where people sat eating breakfast. And my cousin Judith's English class, where the children kept asking me, "You are Jewish. Why don't you live in Israel?"

I circled a strand about the West Bank. I remember traveling through the Arab villages in a brand new Pontiac with my cousin Elieazer. I remember little Arab children throwing stones and spitting at us. My other cousin, Meir, turned to me and said, "We've given them electricity and running water. What more do they want?" An Uzi machine gun sat between his knees. That night I dreamt about men wrestling in sewers as voices shouted, "This is History."

When I returned to Israel eight years later, my cousins' attitudes had begun to change. It was just after the Lebanon war and there were peace demonstrations and strong criticism of the Army. This time when I went to the West Bank there were no Arab children throwing stones, but modern Israeli settlements. I went to Kefer Daniel, the place where Daniel was thrown into the lion's den. It was sunset and the sprinklers were chattering. An old man was on guard duty. He held the Uzi in front of him and I could see the permanent fear in his eyes.

I think about Daniel and the faith which sustained him. I think of this frightened man waving the gun. I think of the most recent eruptions of violence on the West Bank. I want to write about this but I don't really know exactly why. Without the cluster, I wouldn't have discovered it.

Robert Frost describes the dawning of a poem: "It begins as a lump in the throat, a homesickness, a lovesickness. It is never a thought to begin with. It finds its thought and succeeds, or it doesn't and comes to nothing." Clustering is a way to search for the lumps in your throat that want to be uncovered and figured out on the page. Keep it in your toolbox to use along with freewriting and brainstorming.

BL

Follow Through

Look over your cluster and find a provocative strand. Freewrite for ten minutes about it. Circle new information that came to you as you wrote. Choose a new nucleus from this writing and try clustering again. Practice making as many strands as you can from a single nucleus. Remember the best material often comes when the fuel gauge reads empty. Don't be afraid of the blank page staring at you.

Day Seven:
Going Out on Limbs

Today we'll begin with another cluster, but this time choose your nucleus word from one of the lists provided—an idea, a feeling, or a thing—or choose one of your own. Just select a word for the core of your cluster that you think might be a good trigger.

Ideas: religion, success, competition, justice, evil, family, friendship, aging, nature, birth, parenting, politics, education, war.
Feelings: afraid, angry, insecure, joyful, strong, lonely, loving, forgiving, happy, sad, depressed, prejudiced.
Things: cars, trees, water, fire, guns, toys, money, houses, flowers, clothes.

Remember the principles of clustering. Put your nucleus word in the center of a blank page and circle it. Build as many branches as you can, circling what you write and connecting them with lines as you go along. Concentrate on images, names, feelings, code words, ideas, sounds, smells, specific details, whatever comes to mind. The key is to relax and have fun. The harder you try to be "creative," the harder it will be to do it. Ready? Center your nucleus word. Begin clustering from that core. Stop after seven minutes.

Seeing What You Said

Does clustering work for you?

Does any one branch seem especially significant? Are there recurrences—ideas, phrases, details, images that appear several times? Do any branches seem to contradict each other? Do any branches seem closely related? Is there a circled item within a branch that may be a trigger for writing?

Writer to Writer

No technique seems to mimic the way my mind works when I'm talking to a trusted friend better than clustering. I rarely have neatly linear conversations when I really get going. More often I lurch from subject to subject, happily ignoring the lack of logic. I don't mind that while we were chopping wood, Barry commented about how poorly basswood burns in the woodstove and it made me think of a botany class I had many years ago when I fell in love with a dark-haired woman named Linda. The things we say to each other often spark a quick cluster of questions, memories, images, ideas, that often seem only loosely related.

Clustering allows me to cover a lot of ground without worrying about sticking to the straight and narrow. Like brainstorming or freewriting, it's a way to begin thinking about a subject and a way to find my way to other subjects I never would have thought of. And like the other techniques, sometimes it doesn't help at all.

This exercise reminds me of how clustering can help me play with big, unwieldy ideas, and make them my own by anchoring them to the specifics of my past and my present. Writers as a rule do not begin with abstraction. (Try composing a definition of love; it will drive you crazy.) Writers begin (as we have done in all the exercises so far) with the details of what they see or have seen, and *find* the ideas they want to express in the process of trying to make sense of their experience. Here I used clustering to start with the general—cars—to lead me back to the specific—the slightly sweaty smell of the vinyl in the used VW Squareback I owned in college, with its cracked block and ecology sticker on the back.

In America, cars are often fused to our psyches in odd ways (perhaps especially to male psyches). The word *car* is loaded for me, opening the gates to

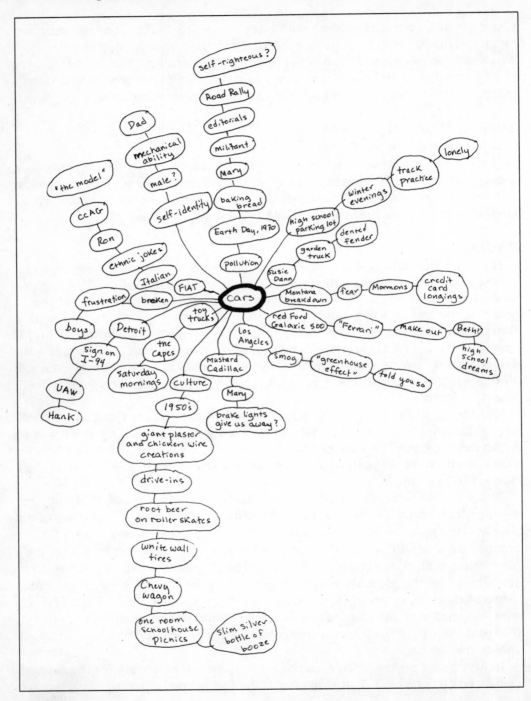

memories of first sex, high school football games, high-pressure car dealers, and breaking down on an empty two-lane highway in Montana.

My cluster is shown on the facing page. Several things intrigue me about what I see here. One branch reminded me of an ideological hatred of automobiles I developed in college, when, soon after the first Earth Day, I pushed to ban weekend road rallies from the campus parking lots. I thought they caused unnecessary air pollution. My columns in the college newspaper on the controversy were bitter, passionate, and self-righteous — three qualities I wore proudly, like an armband, in those days.

Another branch had only three words: "broken," "frustration," and "boys." Those code words remind me that I always seem to be repairing the cars I own, and they are often worse after I'm done with them. Yet male pride somehow prevents me from giving up when my ineptness with a wrench gets me into trouble. That's an angle I want to pursue.

Discovering those angles is one of the great benefits of clustering, when it works. Each branch is potentially another way to see the same subject, and that hunt for fresh angles on familiar material is, as you will see, a crucial part of the writing process.

BB

Follow Through

Set your cluster aside for now. Get up from your writing desk, go outside, and find a small rock. (If you can't find a rock, any small, natural object will work: a twig, piece of bark, flower, etc.) Return to your notebook and spend five minutes making a list of brief observations of the rock. When you look at it, what do you see? What do you think of? Make the list as long as you can. You'll make use of it tomorrow.

Day Eight:
Breaking Habits of Seeing

Return to the list of observations of the rock (or other natural object) you made yesterday. Read it over, then circle any observations that are controversial, *that wouldn't be immediately obvious to someone else looking at your object.*

Be tough on yourself. Don't circle anything unless you really think it's a way of seeing the rock that is unusual.

Seeing What You Said

Are just a few things circled?

Did you find that the vast majority of your observations were obvious, or did you discover that you were able to see your object in some fresh and original ways?

Writer to Writer

Very few objects are more familiar to my writing students than New Hampshire granite. In the beginning, their observations always dwell on physical characteristics: the color of the rock, its shape, its size and weight, its hardness. Sometimes they also mention the rock's uses: the fact that it's easy to throw, will scratch a tabletop, and can pave a driveway. Rarely, someone with a geology background will mention that it contains feldspar and mica and can give off radon gas. Even more unusual are observations that rocks such as these are the curse of New England farmers, or that they form the foundations of the oldest houses, and are common in familiar stone walls whose construction is nearly a lost art. No one yet has noticed that they are objects formed by heat and pressure in an age so distant that it boggles the mind, and that some of the same rock lies in Africa because the two continents once were joined.

Frequently, when my students review their lists of observations for something to circle, they find little that they've noticed about the rock that isn't immediately obvious. For the most part, they see what they've seen before.

A rock is an ideal object for this exercise because it *is* so commonplace. Most writers write about things equally familiar — the thrill and horror of adolescence, coming to terms with the death of a grandparent, the budget deficit, the joys and sorrows of childrearing, or a memorable trip to Paris. All of these subjects have been written about before.

What makes familiar things worth writing about is that we are able to find a way to see them that makes them new, both for us and the people we write for.

When I write about cars, I'm not interested in writing another vague and abstract essay on how important the automobile is in American culture. I'm not interested in simply retelling the tale about the time I backed into a garden truck and dented the fender while waving goodbye to my high school sweetheart, Susie Dann, just to point out again how lovestruck a teenager can be. I already know that.

I *would* be interested in finding out how that first accident at Susie's house might have fit into a pattern of adolescent catastrophes if it would reveal something new about how it felt to be me back then. I *would* be interested in writing about my tangle with the campus Road Rally club if it would help me to understand why I had such a blind passion for saving the world from the environmental crisis. I *would* be interested in writing about the first time I had sex in the back seat of the mustard-colored Cadillac if it would resurrect some image of that scene I had long ago forgotten.

I would be interested in writing about anything, if I can find a way of seeing it through writing that surprises me, that makes the familiar new, *that goes beyond the obvious.* I know that if it surprises me, then it will likely surprise my readers as well.

To write well, we have to learn to see beyond the granite's obvious features. We have to learn to see the old stone walls and the calloused hands that built them, or maybe the movement of continents that brought that rock to our own hands and made us wonder.

BB

Follow Through

Like giving up smoking, breaking habits of seeing is not easy. Clustering (like brainstorming and freewriting) can help because it makes it more likely that we'll accidentally find new angles on familiar subjects. Believe it or not, the camera can help too.

Try this:

Put a fresh roll of film in your camera (any camera, no matter how simple or fancy, will do). Go outside and, in fifteen minutes, shoot the entire roll of one inanimate object, *making each shot different* by varying the angle and distance. If you've got more time, try shooting your object in different light conditions throughout the day. Choose an object that is familiar to you: your house or apartment building, the tree outside your bedroom window, the statue in the park, your car.

Don't worry if you don't know much about photography.

After you've finished, freewrite for five minutes in your notebook about the experience of taking the pictures.

What was difficult about it? What was easy?

Drop the film off to be processed. We'll talk about the results on Day Sixteen.

Day Nine:
Slicing Open the World

Go to a public place with your journal. It should be some place you go to often but never really notice: a shopping mall, a supermarket, a McDonald's, a bank. Sit there for ten minutes and brainstorm a list of details that describe the place. As with the rock exercise, be sure to let your pen wander from a straight physical description to other details which may have more to do with your thoughts, feelings, and associations about the place. Try to use all five senses. Let your list grow quickly. Don't censor words or thoughts. And try not to worry if people are staring at you. Ready? Begin.

Look at your list and circle those details that go beyond the obvious, that say something unique or surprising about the place. If there aren't any, try brainstorming another list from memory and look again.

Take these few best details and write a brief description of the place. Write quickly and don't worry about grammar or punctuation.

Seeing What You Said

Did your list of details grow quickly or did you find yourself staring into space or daydreaming to the Muzak?

Which of the five senses does your list most often engage?

Was it easier to find details that go beyond the obvious in a place than it was with your rock?

What new things did this exercise help you to notice about the place you observed?

Did your description come easily or did you have to struggle to put the information into sentences?

Do your words imply how you feel about the place or are they more objective and impersonal?

Writer to Writer

Once, on a bus to Boston, I asked a woman sitting next to me to point out the building where she worked. "It's the tall one," she said, pointing to the skyline as the bus pulled over the Tobin Bridge. "Could you be a little more specific?" I asked.

"It's the fourth one in."

"I see," I said, trying to figure out if it was the fourth one in from the land or the water or the sky. She noticed the puzzled look on my face and finally said, "It's that silly-looking one that looks like an air traffic control tower." I immediately saw the gawky concrete frame of the Federal Reserve Building with its chicklet-shaped windows towering above the city.

The more we struggle to describe something, the more we move beyond our vague habits of seeing to something more conscious, personal, and truly descriptive. Interestingly enough, the woman's most descriptive detail is the one that tells me a little bit about how she feels about the building. It's silly there, standing on its concrete legs above Back Bay. Maybe in her heart she feels the same way about her job or the commuter lifestyle she has adopted.

In *Writing Down the Bones*, Natalie Goldberg compares writing to baking. "You have all the ingredients, the details of your life, but just to list them is not enough. 'I was born in Brooklyn. I have a mother and father. I am female.' You must add the heat and energy of your heart."

When I go to the mall as a shopper, I stumble through the chaos to find the desired items, I buy them, and escape to my car as soon as possible. But when I go there as a writer, the mall is a river of light and sound and smells that my pen can barely keep up with. There's the sad oregano tinge of pizzas at Papa Ginos, a mother mopping ice cream from a toddler's chin, a patch of sun slipping through the skylight and landing on the face of an old man in a gray fedora, sitting with his hands clasped across his cane. Teenagers laugh above the drowsy violins and the electronic mantras chant over and over in pulsating pagan rhythms from the video parlor. This is a city under glass with air and people constantly pumped in and out, and I am here, right in the middle, with my pen and journal.

In grade school I was taught that details were like wallpaper which writers used to pretty up the page. We were told to write what was known as the "descriptive essay," and the more details we heaped in, the higher our grade. Only years later, through my own writing, did I realize that details were more walls than wallpaper. They build a world in the process of describing, and more importantly, they make that world come alive for both the writer and the reader.

Look at your best details in this workout and you gain insight into how you see the world, and that is different than how I see the world, or Bruce sees the world. When we break our habits of seeing, a truer, more unique vision emerges.

I had a friend who took a watercolor course taught by a Zen Buddhist. For ten weeks they were required to bring a grapefruit to each class, slice it open, smell it, and begin to paint. The results were startling. There were bloody, juice-spitting grapefruits; dry, clothy grapefruits; grapefruits with crystal cores; grapefruits that seemed to dissolve into the page; grapefruits that festered right there in front of you. The teacher had a curious concept of revision. Whenever a student asked him if he should rework a painting, the teacher would nod and say, "Of course, but in another painting."

Search for details that make the world fresh. Think of yourself sitting down with your grapefruit each time you pick up a pen. Slice open the world with a jackknife and stick your nose into it. What do you smell? What do you see?

BL

Follow Through

Brainstorm for ten minutes a list of details to complete a paragraph beginning with this sentence: He/she had a strange taste in clothes.

Let your imagination go wild with specific details. For example, don't just say, "a black belt," but, "the patent leather belt with the polka dot inseam and the commemorative JFK buckle." Have fun!

After you're done, look through your list and circle the telling details which begin to show the world through your own eyes.

Day Ten:
Climbing and Diving

Look at the photograph on the right and imagine for a moment that you are the woman depicted. Go back to the place you wrote about yesterday (or anywhere else you choose) and freewrite for ten minutes about that place through this woman's eyes. Brainstorm first, if you like.

Read over what you wrote. Circle areas you like, things that surprised you. Step back a minute and write one word which describes the mood of this

woman. Place this word at the top of a page and freewrite another ten minutes about this word, drawing as many associations as you can.

Seeing What You Said

Which details in the photo best describe the word you chose? Can you think of more details that would carry on the description?

Can you think of different words to describe the woman's mood?

Did your freewrite on the word bring up any thoughts or memories that surprised you? Which step of the workout did you feel the most comfortable doing? the least?

Writer to Writer

You want to write about your first year of school, but where do you begin? Do you start by describing the smell of pencil shavings, or do you reflect about your fear of the teacher? Do you write about the time Rodney Pinkam wet his pants or your intimidation at marching single file to the toilet with Miss Garland the tank-like first grade teacher? Do you mourn the failure of the American educational system, or do you simply describe the hours spent coloring in the bonnets and hats of pilgrims? Do you write about the nitty-gritty of a particular experience, or do you climb above it and write about the larger patterns?

I came up with a model for illustrating this part of the writing process (shown on the following page). It's called the Ziggurat of Perception and the Sea of Experience.

Many years ago, the story goes, the people of Babel, who all spoke one language, decided to build a tower or ziggurat up to God so they could attain godlike wisdom. But God got angry at the people's false pride. He crumbled the tower and divided the people into many languages.

I speak Barry. Bruce speaks Bruce. You speak you. But when we write, we begin to climb above the nitty-gritty details of our lives and use our wisdom to trace the larger patterns which connect us with all humanity. In the first part of this exercise, you began in the sea of experience, viewing your place through this woman's eyes. When I asked you to stand back and interpret the woman's mood, you began to climb the ziggurat and saw an abstract pattern on the waves beneath. By picking a word like "sadness," you reflected on what you'd done in the flurry of uncritical freewriting.

In the third part of this exercise, maybe you dove into the sea again with a particular memory which attached itself to that word, or maybe you climbed again and reflected even more. Maybe you remembered a woman you met years ago begging for change at a bus station in Boston, or you started wonder-

ing about the nature of sadness and its connection to family relationships in your own life.

Writing is a two-fold process. We dive into the sea of experience, writing details, sounds, smells. We become children experiencing the world for the first time. Then we grow up. We stand back, look for patterns and associations in the chaos of experience, and begin to make sense of it all.

Of course, there is no inherent order to the diving and climbing, and when writing is going well, it almost seems like we are diving and climbing simultaneously. The dangers come when we get too caught up in either occupation.

If we climb the ziggurat too high, we can get stuck in the clouds of general and godlike truth. We write the bland essays Bruce talked about on Day Eight: essays with first sentences like "Cars, everybody has them," or "Death is a very common phenomenon." We need to see through the clouds to our own particular patterns. We need to follow E.B. White's advice and not write about humanity, but about a man.

But we mustn't plunge too deep into particulars and detail and lose track of a larger purpose. The grade school "descriptive essay" begins something like: "The sky was blue. The trees were green. The earth was dappled with yellow light." The reader falls asleep. But if the writer climbs the ziggurat a little and begins something like: "It was my first time alone in the forest. The sky was blue, the trees were green. The earth was dappled with yellow light. Suddenly the sky is much bluer, the trees greener."

By climbing the ziggurat, the writer creates a frame of interest in the reader's mind. The details begin to fill in the curiosity. What was it like to be alone in the forest for the first time? How old were you? How did you end up there? Did someone abandon you like Hansel and Gretel? The writer is no longer writing a descriptive essay, but is describing an experience of vital importance and in the process trying to figure it out.

So far in this book, Bruce and I have encouraged you to dive into the sea of experience. We've taught you how to freewrite, brainstorm, and cluster so that your pen can learn to uncritically remember and rediscover what it was like to be a child and see the world in close detail and in a fresh way. Now it's time to invite your adult voice, or your Watcher, back into the room. It's time to climb the ziggurat and see the larger patterns of the waves beneath.

A good way to begin training your Watcher is to ask yourself questions as you reread your work. Here are a few.

Where do I need to plunge in deeper with more details? Where do I need to climb with more reflection?

Where can I cut away some clouds of general thought and home in on what I really know, or want to know, about the subject?

Where could I freewrite, brainstorm, or cluster to dig for more details or develop my thinking?

BL

Follow Through

Write about a dramatic childhood experience in the first person present tense, as if you are a child. Example: "I sit in the chair. The dentist moves toward me." Brainstorm, cluster, or just dive right in and freewrite for ten minutes. Take the time to settle down. Let yourself slip into your childlike skin. Begin.

Read over what you wrote, then freewrite for another ten minutes as an adult, being in some way critical of the experience. Example: "I never knew the meaning of fear until I took my first trip to the dentist."

Day Eleven:
More Climbing and Diving

Return to the Dorothea Lange photograph "Migrant Mother" in Day Ten and set it before you. Look at it carefully and then spend five minutes freewriting your reaction to the image. Start anywhere with your freewrite, but try to remain somewhat focused on what you see and what the picture makes you feel and think.

Next, read over your freewrite, paying attention to words, lines, or passages that seem to reveal your dominant impression of the photograph. Skip a few lines in your journal and write, in a word, the feeling or idea this photograph communicates to you.

Skip a few more lines. Return to your initial freewrite and the photograph itself, and make a list of details that you think contribute to the one-word feeling or idea you wrote above. Spend a few minutes making as long a list of details as you can.

Finally, circle one detail that you think *most reveals* your dominant impression of the photograph.

Seeing What You Said

Was it hard to write a one-word impression of the photograph? Did you notice new things in it when you made your list of details? Did your impression change after seeing these new details? If someone asked you to explain your impression of the photo, could you? Does your revealing detail say it best?

Writer to Writer

On the wall in my office is one of Barry's drawings (pictured on the facing page), titled "Good and Evil Angels Struggling for the Possession of a Child" (after the William Blake painting). Occasionally my students will notice it, and with pinched eyebrows they will stare and sometimes wonder aloud about its meaning. "Who did that?" they ask. Now and then they will get up from the chair and look again more closely, and suddenly their foreheads will clear in recognition and delight.

I find that moment of recognition—of making sense out of something that seemed to make no sense—is one of writing's greatest joys. But first I plunge into Barry's sea of experience, and, through fast writing, swim like mad hoping to find things that make me wonder. That's exactly what happened to me when I did this exercise. I have always been an admirer of Dorothea Lange's photography. I had seen this photograph, "Migrant Mother, Nippomo, California, 1936" (Library of Congress), many times before. It moved me, but I wasn't sure why or how, and couldn't begin to explain it to anyone else.

In my initial freewrite I found myself writing about the textured landscape of the woman's forehead, with its convergence of horizontal and vertical lines. They were not deep enough to simply betray aging or long hours under a bare sun. I saw instead the lines of a life fractured by worry and despair. Then I noticed the position of her hand on her face, pressing in on her cheek, in a gesture that seemed to say "What next?" As I continued to write, I noted other things: her ragged sleeves, the two older children's dresses cut from the same plain cloth as their mother's, a child's tight fist, and the oblivious, sleeping infant. But most revealing of all, it seemed to me, were the woman's eyes. They reflected no consciousness of the photographer, who must have stood only a few feet away, and little awareness of the children that surrounded her. Instead, her gaze seemed locked on something distant, something out of reach. Those eyes betrayed a feeling of a permanent and deeply private loss.

I suddenly became a witness to that loss in a way I never had before; the photograph took on a fresh, powerful meaning for me. I realized I had seen that look before. On a Lake Michigan beach, I had watched as a northeaster slowly, inevitably destroyed a wooden sloop, run aground on a sandbar, while its owner stood silently watching from the shore. He had those eyes. And so did I, as, years later, I watched my father slowly poison himself with alcohol.

These wonderful, painful moments of recognition are like those of my students looking at Barry's drawing on the wall in my office. First there is uncertainty and confusion, and then a pattern emerges that begins to makes sense. First we plunge into the sea of experience and then tentatively climb the ziggurat of perception, reflecting on what we have seen, and plunge back in again with our new knowledge to see even more.

This exercise mimics Barry's metaphor by asking that you do exactly that—swim and climb, swim and climb—until Dorothea Lange's photograph takes on a personal meaning that is understandable to you. Then, using the specifics of what you see, you can make it understandable to someone else.

Writers do that, moving back and forth between the seeming chaos of information collected and then reflecting on its significance, looking for connections, contradictions, questions, or even specific details—like the migrant woman's eyes—that will reveal meaning.

BB

Follow Through

Using your freewrite, your list of details, and any insights you gained about the meaning of the photograph, compose a paragraph that would explain to someone else how you interpret Lange's image.

Day Twelve:
Life on Tralfamadore
(Climbing and Diving in Time)

Brainstorm a list of dramatic experiences that only lasted a few minutes or even seconds: a car accident, a moment before a big race, a run down a ski slope. Pick one that stands out. Then close your eyes and transport yourself back there for a minute or two. Ready? Now freewrite for five minutes describing those few moments as vividly as you can. Call on all your senses for this.

Now build a list of periods in your life that may have lasted a few weeks, a few months, a few years—high school, service in the Navy, the summer you drove a VW bus through Afghanistan, the month you worked at McDonald's. Pick one that stands out, then brainstorm or cluster more about it to collect specific memories of that time. Try also to write one word that characterizes your current feelings about that time.

When you are ready, find a blank page in your journal and freewrite for ten minutes about this period in your life.

Seeing What You Said

Which part of the workout did you find easier? Why? Where did you write in the most detail?

When you read over what you've written, can you think of more details to add to either section?

Can you pinpoint the places where you climbed the ziggurat of perception, the places where you dove into the sea of experience?

Writer to Writer

In his novel *Slaughterhouse Five*, Kurt Vonnegut, Jr. describes a race of extraterrestrials called Tralfamadorians whose distinguishing characteristic is their ability to see time as we would see a stretch of Rocky Mountains. They marvel at and pity the poor human beings who are glued to the moment, unable to see the past or the future until it has happened. Their ability to see all history, including the destruction of their planet and their own personal destruction, allows them to choose to dwell in the happier moments, unlike humans who must just take what comes along day by day, hour by hour, minute by minute.

In a way, we become Tralfamadorians when we write. Though we don't really see into the future, our entire past is a stretch of Rocky Mountains and we choose where we want to dwell. We can spend pages describing one second of time, or one paragraph to describe ten years. We can tug the reader down deep into the sea of one important minute, or climb the ziggurat and trace a pattern of decades on the waves beneath.

When I started teaching writing, I became quickly familiar with what was cynically referred to by my colleagues as the "alarm clock essay." It begins with something like: "Bzzzzz. 6:00 a.m., time to get up." By page five the student has begun to explore what they really wanted to write about; but when you ask them why they didn't just start there, they look at you as if you are a Tralfamadorian and say, "Well, it didn't happen that way."

Writing is different than living. In some ways it's easier. I can't, for example, go back and revise breakfast because the sausages gave me heartburn, just as I can't go back to sixth grade and stop myself from pounding Sheldon Smalley in the nose. But when I choose to write about those events I do go back there, and I bring all the knowledge I've gained since. Someone once said, "Writers are the kind of people who drive home from a party thinking of all the things they should have said." When we write we exaggerate, distort, or as my old teacher, novelist John Yount used to say, "We lie a little in order to tell the truth better." Playing with time is a writer's chief lying tool.

For the first part of this workout, I wrote about the time my 1964 Volvo rolled over an embankment and into an insurance company's parking lot. I wrote about the five seconds when I turned around, saw what was happening, and lunged for the chrome door handle as the tires went over the crest of the hill. I see those few seconds like a film in slow motion. But as a writer, I have an advantage over any filmmaker because my words can re-create, not only the sights and sounds of those few moments, but everything I was feeling and thinking and have thought and felt since. I see the dusty blue body of the car sliding like a great ship into the ocean on its maiden voyage. I watch my pale fingers grasp the door handle. I listen to the gravel splutter beneath the tires. I'm aware that I have no car insurance; I'm aware that my license will be revoked for three years. I'm aware of the knotted feeling in my chest as I realize the car is moving too fast for me to open the door. Was I aware of all that at the time? I don't really know. But my pen knows what it needs to say.

In the second half of the workout I wrote about junior high. I see myself peering into a mirror with a tube of Clearisil at the ready. I remember the look on Betty Cavannah's face when she turned to me in the lunchline and said, "You wear white socks. You're queer." Her nose squinched up like a crumpled soda can and her eyes turned to tiny slits. I remember how she said the word *queer*, as if it were a little dart she had flung at me. Back then, to be queer, to be odd, was the greatest terror. We were all struggling so hard to be exactly like each other, to be cool. I wanted to be like my friend John Manning, so I bought navy blue turtleneck sweaters and flared Wrangler jeans because he didn't like Levis. A year ago, when I was first married, my wife Carol-lee asked me why I always wore such dark, unflattering colors. With a little horror, I realized I was still trying to dress like Johnny Manning fifteen years later.

I began writing about that group of moments filed away in my memory as junior high, but when I took that chunk of time and, like a lump of clay, started molding it with everything I've known since, I saw that I was writing about conformity and how old patterns hang on if we don't pay attention to our history. When we climb the ziggurat and trace the waves beneath, we begin to discover what we really think about past moments. We become our own personal historians, making new associations, interpreting our lives in surprising ways. And, as Bruce says, when we are surprised, it follows that our readers will be surprised too.

Tralfamadorians aren't surprised about anything. They've seen it all, and ultimately, that is why they are a more boring race. This poem by Philip Levine is about a moment in childhood when his father picked him up and held him against the stars; but it is also about everything he has thought and felt since. Read it slowly, then read it again. Circle the places where Levine dives into the moment, then circle the places where he climbs the ziggurat with everything he's learned since. Stop and think about how amazing it is to be human.

BL

Starlight

My father stands in the warm evening
on the porch of my first house.
I am four years old and growing tired.
I see his head among the stars,
the glow of his cigarette, redder
than the summer moon riding
low over the old neighborhood. We
are alone, and he asks me if I am happy.
"Are you happy?" I cannot answer.
I do not really even understand the word,
and the voice, my father's voice, is not
his voice, but somehow thick and choked,
a voice I have not heard before, but
heard often since. He bends and passes
a thumb beneath each of my eyes.
The cigarette is gone, but I can smell
the tiredness that hangs on his breath.
He has found nothing, and he smiles
and holds my head with both his hands.
Then he lifts me to his shoulder,
and now I too am there among the stars,
as tall as he. Are you happy? I say.
He nods in answer, Yes! oh yes! oh yes!
And in that new voice he says nothing,
holding my head tight against his head,
his eyes closed up against the starlight,
as though those tiny blinking eyes
of light might find a tall, gaunt child
holding his child against the promises
of autumn, until the boy slept,
never to awaken in that world again.

Follow Through

Think about your own father or mother. Cluster or brainstorm about them, trying to dig up moments from your childhood. Pick one moment and freewrite about it for ten minutes.

Look over what you've written and choose one word to describe the overall mood of the writing. Freewrite for another five minutes about that word and how it applies to your relationship with your parent since.

Day Thirteen:
Learning to Love Confusion

Take five minutes or so to wander back into the pages of your journal. Reread some of your favorite entries about experiences, places, or people you have known.

Choose one of these entries, particularly one that you find confusing in intriguing ways or seems to be asking you questions. Answer in freewriting any of the questions below that seem relevant to this entry, encouraging you to reflect on the significance of this person, place, or experience to you now.

If your freewrite stalls on one question, try another.

Keep writing for ten minutes.

What surprised me most about what I said or remembered?

What do I understand now about this that I didn't understand then?

Have my feelings about this (person, place, experience) changed since then? Do I feel differently now?

What do my actions say about the kind of person I was then? How am I different now?

What difference does this make in my life today? Has this person, place, or experience changed the way I think, feel, or act in small or big ways? Is there anything lasting about its significance?

What am I trying to say?

Make up your own question raised by your journal entry: _____
_____ . Try to answer it in a freewrite.

Seeing What You Said

Did any of the questions help bring fresh insight to what you wrote before? Did they raise other questions? Were you frustrated that there weren't always complete answers? Did the entry you reflected on here seem rather cut-and-dried, not particularly significant?

Writer to Writer

"Write about what you know." This cliché is repeated in so many writing books and uttered by so many writing teachers that it has become one of the few great Laws of the craft. I think that's unfortunate, partly because so many young writers take it to mean that they should wait until they are veterans of life, their chests covered with the badges of experience, before they are ready to do serious work.

But what really bothers me about this worn advice is that it can encourage writers to produce their worst work. My students who write slick, air-tight essays about working at McDonald's or skiing slalom usually do it because they know the material so well. It's safe. It's easy. It's also dull to write and dull to read.

I say write about what you *don't* know. Write about what you haven't figured out. Write about what makes you curious. Write about what confuses you. Learn to seek out confusion, draw it close like an injured bird, and with your pen write your way to understanding.

I find it dull to retell old stories that no longer raise questions for me. Like my students whose essays stick to known territory, there are moments in writing this book when I find myself explaining things that I have explained many times before, things that I have come to understand so well that the words arrange themselves on the page. In those moments I feel more like the telephone than the voice, moving the current through the wires, and the writing seems equally as lifeless.

Two years ago, soon after I married Karen, I went to her grandmother's house in Connecticut for the family's annual summer picnic. When we arrived, the yard was filled with sons and daughters, and their sons and daughters, and all the rest of us who were bound to them by love. I had never been to a large family picnic before. My own family viewed such gatherings as a chore, an exercise in diplomacy that attempts—often futilely—to ignore fundamental differences in values, personalities, and interests. Somehow, sharing the same blood or surname didn't seem to matter, and we remained strangers to each other.

I noticed immediately that the clan gathered in Grandma Pouliot's yard that day was as diverse as mine, yet somehow they came together at the same time each August, some traveling hundreds of miles to do it. I wondered why. What was it about this family that allowed them, at least once a year, to overcome indifference?

Moments like these make me wonder. It is those moments that drive me to my journal. I write to learn.

That's exactly what I did the day after the picnic. On the following two pages you can see pages of my journal from which an essay about what holds this family together grew. First, I dove into my sea of experience and quickly wrote a poem (something I rarely do), re-creating some of the images and details I carried away from that afternoon on Grandma Pouliot's lawn. Several lines surprised me. I paused for a moment to gain some distance on the piece, then found the question that seemed to focus my thinking and plunged back into the draft. Over the next few days the essay was coaxed onto the page. Whenever I got stuck, I dove back into freewriting, talking with myself about what I was trying to say, always on the lookout for the questions that would push me further into the draft.

The process involved both of my internal voices — the child and the critic — and by the time I was done, I understood more about what binds the Pouliot clan together once a year on an August afternoon.

Barry and I have talked a lot about these voices so far, first encouraging you to free the child and silence the critic, and then to negotiate an alliance between the two.

This exercise, like those in the few days that preceded it, asks that you bring both selves to your work. Let that intuitive, childlike part of you pursue the things you've seen or remembered or heard that you don't fully understand. Then let your internal critic find the questions that will help you reflect on the significance of those things, which will tell you what it is you want to know.

Don't worry if the questions you have about your subjects raise even more questions, and don't ever think that the answers you come to will be complete, or will not change tomorrow. Our lives are not easily understood, nor are they static. It is enough that we share, through our writing, the little understandings we come to, as I did when I realized that what draws seventy sons and daughters and cousins and their spouses and lovers to Grandma Pouliot's yard every summer is not obligation, but a renewal of the sense of who they are. That's Mrs. Pouliot's gift to them all.

BB

Follow Through

Try brainstorming a list of things you think you could never write about because they seem too painful, or confusing, or unclear. Pick one and write

P. 510

8-18-86

<u>Summer's family reunions</u>

The summoning of names, of lawn chairs,
  of prayers for no rain.
The tribe gathers in the light of afternoon,
  and the smoke of barbecues.
The old, the young, the better forgotten.

"The grandmother looks pale,"
  said in the hush of the old elm,
where starlings gather quietly.
But the chicken pot pie cools in the kitchen,
made by the pale hands with help from daughters.
And the men nod with pleasure over
  their poker hands.
It was always plain pie but it is made.

There are nameless children at games
  but their faces bear the mark of the daughters.

What will keep everyone interested in each other if
it isn't renewing their connection to each other through
this gentle woman, with her gallery of family
photographs, her chicken pot pie, the feel of her
grasp at the back of the neck?

p. 514

8-19-88

   I'm circling this piece without finding out what it is I'm trying to say. I think I've set up an ending where I have to describe what it is that holds this family together that was missing from mine, that makes me want to belong. I also think I've started to say that it is Grandma Pouliot, that she is the family center, the tribal leader who reminds everyone of who they are. There is entropy to the American family. As we define ourselves outside of the family, we lose interest in it. But what happens at these picnics is that the interest is renewed, through her. <u>Despite all the differences, Grandma Pouliot remains a living representative of their collective past.</u>

   I've said all this, and it hardly seems that poignant or new? I haven't answered the "so what?"

   So... family is the one thing we'll always belong to, and it provides a continuity that's so often missing from our lives, and it does tell us who we are by helping us to understand where we've come from. The family picnic is a celebration of this connection, a <u>ritual of belonging.</u>

   What overcomes the apathy? The longing to know again who we are? Ugh....

your way into it for five minutes, starting anywhere. Sometimes the things that we try to keep at arm's length are the things we most want to understand.

Gathering the Clan at Grandma's Picnic

I am the new husband of the daughter of a daughter and now I am expected to be seen at the annual August family picnic in Coventry. Grandma Pouliot, who presides over these events, grabs the back of my neck as I lean down to kiss her, and with a strength that surprises me, presses my cheek to hers.

It means, I think, that I am now considered a member of the tribe.

It is a big group, gathered there in the shade of beech and maple trees. Justine Pouliot, 86, had thirteen children, most of them daughters, and every summer in late August many of them return to her small, white frame house on a quiet street in the Connecticut countryside. They bring barbecue food and beer and boyfriends and the new children who now extend the family further.

The new husbands and boyfriends eye one another sympathetically. We don't know one another's names, but nod in passing, aware that we are new initiates in this ritual of belonging. One day we may be invited to join the older men at the poker table under the tree at the far end of the yard.

But it is Grandma Pouliot's strong embrace when we arrive that makes me feel I belong here. And when she invites me to enter her house to look at the family pictures that cover the walls of every room, I search for our own wedding picture, expecting to find it easily.

"We did send it to her?" I ask my wife, Karen. "I think so," she says.

We never do find it, though Karen assures me it's there on some unseen wall or shelf. I wander back out to the yard wishing I would be invited to join the poker game. It is a strange longing, because I dislike cards and am uneasy in the company of men and money.

I sit down on a lawn chair, and while I watch the smoke from barbecues drift through the trees, one of my wife's aunts tells me about the job prospects of each of her sons. She talks as if I know them all, and I pretend I do. As I listen, I think about my own family, small and splintered and living separate lives on both coasts, with a few cousins and uncles still lingering in Chicago, where I was born.

When I was young, we would sometimes gather at Thanksgiving or Christmas. But these family affairs became more sporadic and less joyful as I grew older. It wasn't bitterness that made us drift away from one another, but apathy. We simply lost interest in one another's lives as they took on a meaning separate from the family, and finally we became strangers to one another.

"Don't you think Grandma Pouliot looks pale?" Karen asks. "I've never seen her look so tired."

Grandma is stationed in a rocker lawn chair, being introduced to the new boyfriend of a daughter's daughter. I notice that even he leans down to kiss her before driving off loudly in his glossy blue pickup truck.

Everyone, coming and going, pays respects to Grandma Pouliot, and love for her softens the faces of even the toughest teenagers in the family.

I don't really know whether she looks especially tired or pale this day. But I do think she seems happy as she quietly scans the gathering that fills her yard. I tell Karen this, but I know it doesn't reassure her.

Several times I hear cousins in quiet conversation wonder whether these family picnics will continue after Grandma Pouliot is gone. I wonder too, knowing how easily family members can become strangers without something or someone to remind them of who they are.

I think Grandma Pouliot knows this too, which is why she still goes to every wedding, still remembers every birthday and still rises early every year before the family picnic to make two large chicken pot pies in her small white house full of pictures.

Day Fourteen:
If You Can't Be James Joyce,
Why Bother?

You've been writing for two weeks now. Who cares? I mean, do you really think all this scribbling is going to make any difference? Who would ever be interested in reading things that happened to *you*? Isn't it about time you found a better way to occupy your time? Wouldn't this be a good night to try that new restaurant where they slice the meat at the table? Wouldn't you rather be doing the *Jane Fonda Workout Video*, so you'll live longer and have more to write about ten years from now?

Stop. Find a blank page in your journal and freewrite for ten minutes about all the reasons why you shouldn't write, all the things that discourage you from writing.

Look at your writing. Read it out loud to yourself. Circle the best arguments. Memorize your voice of doubt, so you'll be able to identify it next time it comes to sabotage your work.

Seeing What You Said

Did you find a lot of reasons for not writing, or did this workout seem silly and pointless?

What are your strongest doubts, and are they ever strong enough to stop a day's writing?

What are things you say to yourself to combat doubts? Do they work, or do your doubts go away only when they feel like it?

Are there writers whose work is so good that reading them discourages you? Are there writers whose work is so good it inspires you? Do others write so bad that you're inspired to do better?

What can you do physically to work through an attack of doubt?

Writer to Writer

A literature professor once confided in me that he had written a novel when he was my age and didn't know any better. He told me most literature professors have a novel tucked away in a drawer somewhere, but after a short time they say to themselves, "If I can't be James Joyce, why bother?"

I nodded in agreement. I was young then, and though I knew I wanted to be a writer, I stood in awe of the masters I studied and wrote about. If I could return to his office today as that twenty-one-year-old literature student, I would tell him, "But James Joyce can't be you. For one thing, he's dead; but even if he were still alive, he could not know all the things *you* know or wonder about exactly the same things *you* wonder about. The reason you aren't a novelist is because you stopped writing. You gave up."

All writers struggle with self-doubt, that overpowering urge to believe that everything you have ever written or will ever write is total *dreck*. For some writers it's a daily occurrence; for others it hits after their first book is published or after they've collected enough rejection slips to wallpaper the den. In *Writing with Power*, Peter Elbow calls doubt the writer's demons:

First the demons try to stop you from writing at all. If they fail, then they stop you from making some passages strong. If they fail again, then as a last ditch effort, they try to trick you into thinking what you have is garbage. They try to trick you into either throwing it away in disgust or into taking the whole thing apart again and thereby luring you back into the swamp where you will finally give up in exhaustion.

Elbow recommends giving the feelings of doubt a free rein. Freewrite about how disgusted you are with your writing. The more you can express the doubts, the more you can see them for what they are and not internalize them or confuse them with your helpful Watcher.

Think of your writing as your child. Do you reject your child when you're in a bad mood, or do you say, "I'm in a bad mood right now. I'm tired. Later, I'll be in a better mood." Maybe there are things you can do to change your mood. Go for a short walk. Eat ice cream. Make a cup of coffee and watch the sunrise. Go to Dunkin Donuts and write on the clean Formica countertop while eating french crullers and watching the truck drivers drink coffee.

Writers develop their own methods of dealing with self-doubt. A student once told me, "I love reading John Updike, but whenever I read a story or novel by him, I can't write for days. He's just so damn good." I told her, "If you want to be a writer, stop reading John Updike. Read people who make you want to write. Read Harold Robbins or Leon Uris or Danielle Steel or Barbara Cartland. Read the newspaper."

When the doubting demons come to my house, I turn to a collection of quotes pinned to the corkboard near my desk. Most of the quotes are by writers, and though they are not always profound, they all make me want to write. One of my favorites is by Henry Miller from the first chapter of *Tropic of Cancer*:

There are no more books to be written, Thank God. This then? This is not a book. This is libel, slander, defamation of character. This is not a book in the ordinary sense of the word. No, this is a prolonged insult, a gob of spit in the face of Art, a kick in the pants to God, Man, Destiny, Time, Love, Beauty . . . what you will.

I like this quote because it tells me not to be intimidated by all the great geniuses past and present. It speaks to the creative voice in me that has something to say and will not be hushed by any lofty ears who may be listening. It tells me I don't have to be Shakespeare and that, probably, Shakespeare wasn't trying to be Shakespeare either. He was just another scribbler who happened to write timeless masterpieces.

There are other methods I use to chase away the doubting demons. I like to change tools. I move from the computer back to the old Royal manual typewriter, back to the pen or pencil. I switch from yellow legal pads to wire-bound notebooks to blank sheets of typing paper. I reposition my writing desk to make me feel like I'm starting something new. I think of the inspiring words of my best writing teachers, the poet Ted Walker, and fiction writer Sue Wheeler. I think of my fourth grade teacher, Mrs. Carolyn Foley, the first person to give real recognition to my scribbling. I see her sitting at an upright piano, working the pedals with her spike-heeled shoes. I watch her throw back her head and sing in a high soprano, "I went to the animal fair/ the birds and the beasts were there/the big baboon by the light of the moon/was combing his auburn hair. . . ."

Right at this moment my wife Carol-lee has entered the bedroom closet where I am writing this. She reminds me that the radiator on the truck is shot, there's no wood for the woodstove, the pipes in the bathroom have frozen and burst, and our three-year-old daughter Jessie has just unraveled several spools of thread throughout the house. I tell her I'll be with her in a minute and crank up the Bach partitas on the boom box. For a moment, I turn to a quote from a story by fiction writer David Evanier, which hangs over my computer. I'm not sure why I find it inspiring at moments like this, but I do. "If you want to be a writer don't expect anything for it. Don't want anything. Get a job. Get a family. Just do it before you die or get off the pot."

BL

Follow Through

Here are a few ways to combat the demons of doubt. Try any that may be of help to you.

Look through your own books or go to a library. Seek out authors who feed your desire to write. Remember, these writers won't necessarily be your favorite authors, or even ones that you like. Make a list of them and keep a few of their books near your writing area. Love them or loathe them, these writers will remind you, any time your confidence sags, that words on a page matter.

Make a list of all your best writing experiences. Keep it in your journal as ammunition when doubts strike.

Read interviews with other writers (the *Paris Review* interviews are particularly good) and copy down quotes that make you want to write. Read the classics or the comics, whichever inspires you more.

Acknowledge your moods. Know the difference between your Watcher and your demon. If you sense yourself being overly critical, stop. Lower your standards or work on something else.

Day Fifteen:
The Magic Flashlight

By now you've generated a lot of material and begun exploring your power as a writer to dive into past moments, or to climb above and trace the larger patterns on the waves. You know not only how to scribble, but how to stand back from your scribbling and look for discoveries and telling details. You've begun to get a feel for what your richest subjects are and how to probe them through questions, freewriting, brainstorming, and clustering. You're probably saying to yourself, "Now I want to write something, but where do I begin?"

A "lead" is a term coined by journalists because it leads the reader, and the writer, into a piece of writing. It is not an introduction, because it does much more than introduce. It sets a tone, raises questions in the reader's mind, and gives focus to writers grappling for angles on unwieldy subjects. A lead can be one sentence, a few paragraphs, or even a page. Non-fiction writer John Mc-Phee calls leads "flashlights that shine down through a story. They are not just the first words of a piece but the integral beginning that sets the scene and implies the dimension of the story."

Look over your work for Day Thirteen, or any other day that produced material you want to work with. Do a cluster diagram about your subject and compose five to ten short leads (a sentence or a short paragraph) to an essay based on different branches of the cluster. Write quickly and don't worry if they're good or not. Try starting in the sea or climbing the ziggurat. Let yourself explore all the different places you could begin writing. Ready? Begin.

Look through your leads and pick one that wants to be followed. Freewrite for ten minutes, beginning with the lead you chose. See where it leads you.

Seeing What You Said

Did you find it easy to write leads or did you struggle with the choices?

Did most of your leads begin in the sea or did you climb and reflect?

Did your freewrite come easily or did the lead take you up a blind alley?

Do you see any more leads in the freewriting you did? Were there any other leads you would like to follow? Would it help you to brainstorm or cluster more about your subject to find more leads?

Writer to Writer

Freewriting and other journal writing about a subject can be likened to stumbling down a dark hallway looking for a doorknob to wrap your fingers around. Sometimes all a writer needs is the right first sentence or paragraph, the right lead, and a piece will literally begin writing itself. Short story writer Raymond Carver describes such an experience.

> I once sat down to write what turned out to be a pretty good story, though only the first sentence of the story offered itself to me when I began it. For several days I'd gone around with the sentence in my head: "He was running the vacuum cleaner when the phone rang." I knew a story was there that wanted telling. I felt it in my bones that a story belonged with that beginning, if I could just have time to write it. I found the time, an entire day—twelve, fifteen hours even—if I wanted to make use of it. I did and sat down in the morning and wrote the first sentence, and other sentences promptly began to attach themselves. I made the story just like I'd make a poem; one line and then the next and then the next. Pretty soon I could see a story and I knew it was my story, the one I'd been wanting to write.

Carver's experience is not unusual. A good lead pulls the reader and the writer along, and more than that, it often contains the heart of a piece of writing.

Lets go back to Bruce's essay on page 45 and read his lead paragraph.

> I am the new husband of the daughter of a daughter and now I am expected to be seen at the annual August family picnic in Coventry. Grandma Pouliot, who presides over these events, grabs the back of my neck as I lean down to kiss her, and with a strength that surprises me, presses my cheek to hers.
>
> It means, I think, that I am now considered a member of the tribe.

The first sentence suggests Bruce is going to this picnic simply because he is required to as a new member of the family, but in the second sentence, Grandma Pouliot's strength somehow surprises him and, as a reader, it surprises me too. By the third sentence I ask myself, how does one woman's embrace make you a member of a tribe? What does it mean to be a member of the tribe? And do the other people at the reunion feel the same way as Bruce? All these questions get answered later in the essay when I see that it's Grandma Pouliot's strength that holds an entire family together by telling the lost generations who they are.

Good leads set up expectations in the reader's mind and also, like flashlights, they help writers to see where they are heading. Here are a few of my favorite leads. Read them and listen to the questions they raise in your mind. Then read the source and notice how a lead predicts the content of the pages to come.

I was born in 1927, the only child of middle class parents, both English, and themselves born in the grotesquely elongated shadow, which they never rose sufficiently above history to leave, of that monstrous dwarf Queen Victoria. I was sent to public school, I wasted two years doing my national service, I went to Oxford: and there I began to discover I was not the person I wanted to be.
(*The Magus* by John Fowles. An existential novel about an Englishman searching for his identity.)

He was not to do anything in bad taste, the woman of the inn warned Eguchi. He was not to put his finger in the mouth of a sleeping girl, or try anything else of that sort.
(*The House of Sleeping Beauties* by Yasunari Kawabata. A Japanese novel about an old man who eventually goes against the rules in a bizarre brothel where old men sleep beside drugged virgins.)

As Gregor Samsa awoke one day from uneasy dreams he found himself transformed into a gigantic insect.
(*Metamorphosis* by Franz Kafka. This is a story about a businessman who gets turned into a cockroach but still feels a need to make it to the office.)

I was an untruthful little boy.
("The Story of My Dovecot" by Isaac Babel. A short story about a boy who learns something about truth.)

When I heard that Isaac Kornfield, a man of piety and brains, had hanged himself in the public park, I put a token in the subway stile and journeyed out to see the tree.
("The Pagan Rabbi" by Cynthia Ozick. A short story about a rabbi who was hanged by a wood nymph.)

We tell ourselves stories in order to live.
("On Keeping a Journal" by Joan Didion. An essay about the importance and power of keeping a journal.)

Many years later, as he faced the firing squad, Colonel Aureliano Buendia was to remember that distant afternoon when his father took him to discover ice.
(*One Hundred Years of Solitude* by Gabriel Garcia Marquez. A magical novel where time isn't limited to one moment separated from all the others.)

Call me Ishmael.
(*Moby Dick* by Herman Melville. A novel about a whale told like a biblical prophecy.)

Although I didn't realize it at the time, my mother was getting prettier. My sister was a beauty. My adolescence was the time of our greatest estrangement.
("Competition" by Nancy Friday. An essay about the disturbing estrangement between women of the same family.)

My friend Mel McGinniss is talking. Mel McGinniss is a cardiologist, and sometimes that gives him the right.
(*What We Talk About When We Talk About Love* by Raymond Carver. A story about four drunk people conducting a symposium on love. Note: Mel is the most cynical.)

All this happened, more or less. The war parts, anyway, are pretty much true. One guy I knew really was shot in Dresden for taking a teapot that wasn't his. Another guy I knew really did threaten to have his personal enemies killed by a hired gunman after the war. And so on. I've changed all the names.
(*Slaughterhouse Five* by Kurt Vonnegut, Jr. A novel about the author's attempt to deal with the bombing of Dresden.)

Now, the Star-Belly Sneetches
Had bellies with stars.
The Plain-Belly Sneetches
Had none upon thars.
Those stars weren't so big. They were really so small.
You might think such a thing wouldn't matter at all.
(*Sneetches* by Dr. Seuss. A gripping story about the insanity and powerlessness of those caught up in jealousy.)

Notice how some leads point the reader in a specific direction, where others simply whet the reader's curiosity. Good leads don't have to be sensationalistic but they should encourage the reader to keep reading. Even thick novels often begin with one sentence containing the essence of the pages to come.

In grammar school I was taught that every essay or story must begin with an introduction, an Ed McMahon who stumbled onto the page and announced, "and heeeeeeere's the essay." I was taught that you needed to "say what you're going to say, say it, then say what you already said." It's no wonder everything I wrote was about as compelling as an insurance policy and that, years later when I became a writer, I found myself cutting pages of bland beginnings. A lead is not an introduction to a story, just as birth is not an introduction to life, but the thing itself.

Lately a lead for a strange short story keeps buzzing through my head. It goes something like this: "She had died so quickly she had hardly noticed." That's as far as I've gotten, but I know it's a dream-like story about what it would be like to die and still be alive. It started a month ago when I had a dream about a friend dying and returning to life as a melody that swept through a house like a fresh breeze. I have no idea what the story will be about or whether I will even write it, but I have a feeling it's important and I should try.

This is where a lot of my work begins, with an urgent feeling and a sentence which attaches itself to that feeling and shines a dim light down a corridor black as night.

BL

Follow Through

Try writing fifteen leads to pieces you will probably never write. Leads like: "On a plane thirty thousand feet above the Mediterranean, Blake decided there was more to life than selling candy bars," or "She told him no, but Kirby Price didn't have the two-letter word in his vocabulary."

Write leads to tacky romance novels, leads to mysteries, leads to thrillers, newspaper stories, and autobiographical novels. Remember that writing leads is fun. Be daring. Be sensational. Be cheap. Don't be afraid to grab the reader by the lapels and drag the reader in. Don't forget to enjoy yourself.

Out of your leads pick one or two that are particularly compelling and compose for ten minutes. If possible, try swapping leads with a friend. See what happens when they follow yours and you follow theirs. Remember what Elmore Leonard says: "Writers write for the same reason readers read: to find out what's going to happen."

Day Sixteen:
Twenty Ways to See an Elm Tree

By now, the photographs you took on Day Eight should be back from the processor. Spread them out on your writing desk. Arrange them in front of you, from left to right, from your most favorite to your least favorite images. Eliminate any that failed because of technical reasons such as lack of focus or light or problems with processing.

In your journal, spend a few minutes jotting down what it is about your favorite photograph that made you choose it. Be as specific as possible.

Rearrange them again, but this time begin with the pictures that you think show your subject in the *least obvious way* because of the angle they were shot, the distance from your subject, or the quality of the light.

Now spend five minutes freewriting a response to this question: How did my experience with the process of taking these photographs seem similar to the process of writing?

Seeing What You Said

Did you find that your favorite photographs in step one of this exercise were also your favorites in step two, or were your two arrangements quite different? Did any help you to see your familiar subject in a new way?

Did you have difficulty taking multiple pictures of the same subject, or were you able to snap away like mad? Were the shots you carefully planned as good as the shots you found spontaneously?

Did the meaning of your subject change for you the more shots you took? Could you take another roll of the same subject? Would you want to?

Writer to Writer

Several years ago, I decided to take up photography again. I dusted off my camera, bought a roll of film, and headed out to my favorite ocean beach in Kittery, Maine. It was a cold, wintry day, but the sun was high and strong, as were my spirits. I was certain that this beautiful place would yield a bounty of photographic possibilities. I was wrong.

It's not that the subject matter wasn't there; I just couldn't find it. I spent two hours wandering around with the camera around my neck, hunting for images, feeling silly. I was snapping the shutter at a rate of one picture every twenty minutes, and I was definitely *not* having fun. My disgust finally turned to despair when I found myself carefully composing a picture of a lighthouse that *everyone* seems to take a picture of. I stared through the lens, but I could not bring myself to push the shutter release. I remembered a postcard shot of the same lighthouse from the same angle that was probably, at that moment, making its way through the mail to hundreds of people who would, in a glance, see every lighthouse in Maine they've ever known or imagined.

"Nice going, Bruce," I said to myself. "You found a cliché."

A few days later it dawned on me that I had been mugged by my Watcher on the beach that day. And the more I thought about it, the more I understood that my reluctance to play and experiment with the camera was exactly like my unwillingness to play with the pen. I knew I was on to something, that the process I used to take pictures was remarkably similar to the process I used to write, and that each could help the other.

The next week a storm swept through, and the landscape around my house was transformed by snow. All day I thought about taking pictures. When I finally had time to grab the camera and head out in the dwindling light of evening, I began to see a place I'd never seen before. I saw light and color and texture dancing together in every corner of the pasture, and around the red barn next door, and over at the old Huggins place down the road.

This time, conscious of my tendency to compose and plan every shot, I decided to go slightly mad with the camera, snapping shots with a speed that outran my critical self; I "freewrote" with the camera.

I didn't even have to try. There were suddenly images everywhere, including a series of my cat sitting serenely in soft waves of white snow, tinged with a

wash of red from the setting sun. If I'd thought about it much, I never would have taken those pictures. More than once, I had ruled out pet pictures as trite and sentimental.

But I loved these pictures when they came back from the processor, and it was then I realized that an open-ended immersion into my photographic subjects could yield the same happy accidents I found when writing fast and freely.

The writer always works to go beyond the obvious. A few days ago I talked about how I was able to see not just a family picnic, but also the way in which Grandma Pouliot helps make the event a renewal of the family's sense of self. I experienced the same process when I photographed a dead elm, which stands alone in an empty field in front of my house. Each new picture was a different way of seeing the tree; until then, I thought I'd seen it pretty thoroughly. The shots I liked best were often those that occurred to me only in the madness of taking lots of pictures. I liked this old tree, but always saw it from a distance. In a flurry of picture taking, I got closer and saw things I'd never noticed before: the way it's riddled with woodpecker holes, how it sheds bark like a snake's skin. Writers sometimes circle their subjects the way I circled this tree. Each new shot, like each new draft, helps break our habits of seeing, making a familiar subject new again.

Yesterday, Barry described leads as flashlights that shine into shadowy subjects. Each different lead illuminates a different direction the writing may go, each defines another aspect of the subject. In a sense, the photographs spread before you right now are like leads. Every time you changed the angle, the distance, and the time of day, you might have revealed a different possibility in your subject. My distant shots of the elm tree speak to me of isolation and death, the pictures I shot of the trunk suggest strength and perseverance, and the close-ups of the bark hung loosely remind me of the shedding skin of a snake. Like a good lead, it is that last photograph that I want to follow, and tomorrow I'll return to the tree with my camera and shoot more close-ups, hoping for one image that will make someone else say, "Now look at that!"

I have learned not to completely trust my initial way of seeing things, both in writing and photography. More and more, I put my faith in a process that may yield new ways of understanding. It is this feast of little surprises that, more than anything else, draws me to the journal and typewriter.

BB

Follow Through

Decide which images of your subject begin to say something to you, and then, like a writer who discovers an intriguing lead, return with your camera and take more pictures that develop the idea or feeling you're beginning to discover.

Be open to new possibilities the more you work with your photographic subject. Consider each shot a draft, and each new one a revision. Work towards developing one photograph that you think will communicate something to someone else without explanation from you. Work for an image that might make someone say, "Now look at that!"

Day Seventeen:
The Horse Race of Meaning

Go back to Day Fifteen. Cluster and brainstorm some more or simply pick one of your favorite leads and follow it for ten minutes. Write quickly. Let your pen lead you along.

Look at what you've written. Search for new leads. Pick one, turn to a blank page, and put your lead at the top.

Write quickly for another ten minutes.

Look at what you've written and search for new leads. Find one, put it at the top of a new page. Follow it for another ten minutes.

Seeing What You Said

Was it easy to spot new leads or did you find yourself staring at the sprawling mass? Did you like any of the later leads better than the ones you started with?

How do your different leads approach the subject differently? How do you decide which lead you like better?

Writer to Writer

Whenever you decide to write on a subject you are immediately swamped with a glut of information. How should you write about your grandfather? Do you describe him in detail? Or do you simply tell of the fishing trip he took you on? Do you climb the ziggurat and try to put into words what he meant to you, or do you dive into the room where his coffin lay and describe the nauseating color of the purple wallpaper or your angry feelings? Or maybe you should start earlier, at the camp, where he taught you how to clean a lake trout?

You might look at each piece of writing as a horse race of information, the most important bits taking the lead as you revise. (See the illustration on the following page.) What started as a documentary account of the day of the hurricane may end up as an essay about your feelings of protectiveness toward your little sister and how they've changed through the years. You thought the hurricane was important, but it wasn't until you sat down and wrote that you saw the possibilities of the section where you describe holding your sister and telling her fairy tales in the lantern light. The parts about the hurricane seemed less important as the new story emerged from the pack of information and your lead became, "I remember telling her fairy tales as the shutters pounded in the wind. We huddled under blankets by the oil furnace," instead of, "I will always remember the day of the hurricane."

The horse race begins in our minds, long before we put pen to paper. A student once told me she wanted to write an essay about buying a truck, but she wasn't sure why. After clustering and freewriting, she remembered how her father used to take her for drives in his old truck along back roads on summer evenings. She remembered watching him change the spark plugs, and then feeling resentment toward her two brothers, who used to ridicule her mechanical ability. Today she could do a tune-up better than either of them.

By the time she started writing, her essay was less about buying a truck and more about what it means to be a woman in a male-dominated society. As she writes, her essay may change again. Another horse may pull away from the pack and take the lead.

Look at the favorite photographs you took with Bruce. What visual element has taken the lead? What element has fallen to the rear of the pack? Did you intend to make it the lead, or was it a happy accident you stumbled upon in the fury of shutter snapping?

Did your revisions of the favorite photographs yield a different visual emphasis and eliminate what was central before? If all this is happening, then there is a good chance you are becoming a photographer and will apply the same methods to become a writer.

I've been trying to write that short story I talked about on Day Fifteen—the one that began, "She had died so quickly she had hardly noticed." I had an hour the other morning to sit by the kitchen woodstove scribbling into a spiral-bound notebook.

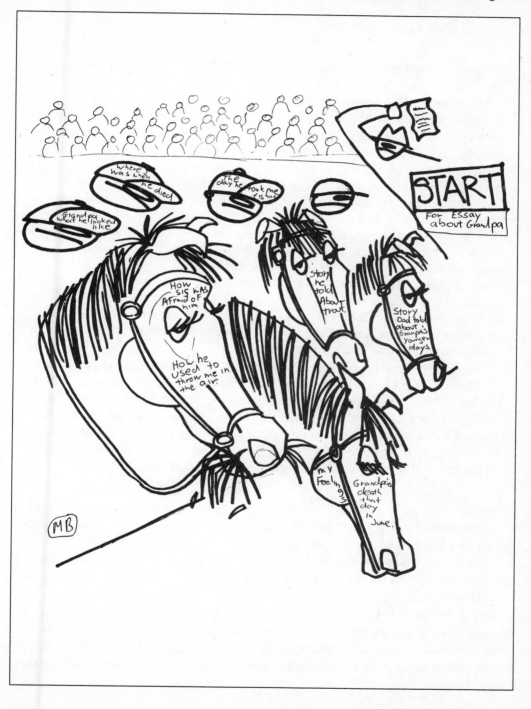

Here's what I came up with:

She had died so quickly she had hardly noticed. She was on her way to the supermarket but suddenly she had no car, no fingers gripping the steering wheel, no legs and arms, no shopping list. She slipped through the glass doors and floated like smoke up and down the aisles. She had never noticed how beautiful the cans and jars were, stacked so neatly on the shelves, and how green was the cellophane grass where the bananas sat heaped in a pile, how the bags of flour puffed out their little chests so proudly. And the people in the supermarket. She could see inside them. She could float past the carts full of beer and Wonderbread into their eyes and see them as children. She could share the joy. It was like stepping through the hard crust of snow to the soft powder beneath or opening a black door and being bathed in warm orange light. That old man who looks so sad, whose eyes are storm shutters closed to winter wind and summer light. The years stretched like old rags over his cheekbones. Look inside and see the young boy running in the summer breeze, a child washed in the clear light of his mother's smile. His breath sweet as candy. His voice a morning lark. They were all prisoners in these bodies, like the groceries trapped in the clanging steel cages.

She was in the soap aisle when she realized she hadn't bought anything, that she couldn't because she was dead. That word like a hoofbeat pounding on the joy which swelled in her. She saw the truck swerve into her path. She heard the screech of the tires, the shattering glass, the sirens wailing like lost souls calling her. Then the rising feeling like a large bird spreading its wings inside her chest. What does it mean to die? She had spent most of her life trying to figure out what it meant to be alive.

That's as far as I got before my three-year-old daughter Jessie came into the room demanding that I peel her an apple and turn on Sesame Street. I noticed the fire had died and there was no wood beside the stove.

I liked what I had written then, but now, as I type it into the book, I find all kinds of faults with it and have to bite my lip to resist editing so you can see exactly what I wrote.

Still, I like the idea of a woman, a mother, being dead yet alive, still in the supermarket. I like how she sees beyond the surface of things, and I'm beginning to wonder about who she really is. There is a feeling in the pit of my stomach which tells me I must write more. Already, I have a few possible new leads.

She was in the detergent aisle at the supermarket when she realized she hadn't bought anything, she had no arms or legs or fingers; she was dead.

She heard the screech of tires, the shattering glass, the sirens wailing like lost souls calling to her.

She slipped through the glass doors of the supermarket and floated like smoke down the aisles.

BL

Follow Through

Close your eyes for a moment and think about the essay or story you plan to write. Now, on a blank piece of paper in your journal, draw a picture of the essay.

Yes, I know you are not an art student. The last time you were asked to draw a picture might have been in the fourth grade by a dowdy art teacher who yelled at you for eating school glue. But for the next few minutes, forget all that. Pretend you are da Vinci and fill the page with the characters and ideas from your story or essay. Don't be embarrassed to draw stick figures. Maybe you're not da Vinci. Maybe you are a caveman or cavewoman, scratching out your vision of the world on the limestone walls. Begin.

Stand back from your drawing and notice what information seems most central, what has drifted to the background. Write a lead which seems to sum up the drawing. My drawing for which the following lead was written is pictured on the next page.

My drawing for the story I am writing is pictured on the next page. It's sort of a map of where the story might end up. The woman is in the sky and her family and friends are at her funeral. Nobody can see her because they are turned away. Only one person can see her. Only one person connects her with the gathering. Who is it? An old lover? A close friend? Her son or daughter? I don't know why I drew this person looking at Claire, but I did. I think Claire needs to be anchored in this world. Until I drew this, I didn't realize this was where I was heading. And though I may not end up there, this silly drawing adds a sense of structure to my journey.

Day Eighteen:
Getting to the Draft

Yesterday you played again with leads. Today, select the one lead to your story or essay that seems most promising to you, and for thirty minutes continue to push it along to the end in your journal. You'll be composing more than free-writing now. Think about what you want to say before you say it.

If you need another day to finish your draft, fine. But don't draw out the process more than one or two days; force yourself to complete a draft quickly, even if that means leaving unsatisfactory holes or loose ends. Don't let your Watcher prevent you from finishing a fast draft.

If you're having problems finishing a draft quickly, do this: take a piece of paper and a magic marker and write three words—"It Doesn't Count." Put it on the wall above your writing desk as a reminder to your internal critic, who may insist that you can't possibly finish your draft because it isn't "perfect."

Seeing What You Said

Did you have to fight your way through to the end of your draft, or could you easily follow the trail established by your lead to a conclusion? Did your Watcher give you hell?

How well did your lead work? Did you discover yet another, better one in your draft? Did anything in the draft surprise you? When you were done, did you feel satisfied with the draft, or were there things you needed to add?

Writer to Writer

One day while freewriting, I reminded myself of a moment long ago. I was eight, and I stood in a darkened control booth at a large television studio in the Merchandise Mart in downtown Chicago. I was watching my mother, an actress, down on the studio floor talking into the camera about the benefits of heating a home with natural gas. She was performing in a live commercial during a break on the evening news, and I remembered watching her with both awe and pride as she stood there awash in white light. I spent many evenings with her in television studios back then, when Chicago was a thriving television town and Mom was a rising star in the medium.

Since then I have often wondered—and often been asked—what it felt like to be the son of someone countless strangers knew by name. I realized that I didn't know, and I wanted to write about it to see if I could find out. Yesterday, at Barry's urging, I tried writing some leads. Here they are:

When I was seven or eight, my mother took me to the Merchandise Mart to put in occasional appearances on a TV show called "Today on the Farm." She was a regular on the program, along with a lanky and whole-some-looking singer named Eddie Arnold. I was enlisted as a generic child, whenever one was needed.

Once, while I was a college student, someone passed along a member-ship card to the Carmelita Pope fan club. It was roughly drawn, hardly official looking, with a picture of two eggs being launched from a frying pan.

I witnessed the early days of Chicago television from the shadows. Stage fright drove me there, after a few brief and speechless appearances in ads promoting natural gas, savings accounts, and kitchen cabinets.

I remember hearing my mother's voice coming from the television in the other room. It was the same voice that she used to talk to my girlfriend's parents or to make doctor's appointments. It was a strange yet familiar voice, and somehow I knew it wasn't meant for me.

I like most of the leads (and I end up using most of them somewhere in the draft), but the first most makes me want to write the second paragraph. I followed it, and in a fast draft tried to find out where it led (see page 167). Perhaps like you, I had to push myself to write my way to the end.

My Watcher always pesters me about awkward sentences, often whispering those two words — "so what?" — that curse many writers too early in the writing process.

When I was done and reread the draft, I cringed at places that seemed dishonest (did I *really* want to be a star?), or overwritten ("an erudite and thoughtful-looking fellow" — ugh), or trite ("very nearly swooned with anticipation"). At first, I was so dissatisfied with the result that I was unable to see that *good* things happened in the draft. Buried on page three was a paragraph that quietly asked me to take notice, and I finally did, after I stopped berating myself for my "bad" writing.

But when I would watch from the darkened control booth as Mom became Carmelita Pope, spokesperson for Illinois Natural Gas Company or Bell Savings, live on the evening news with Alex Drier, I realized that she was talking directly to that dark and forbidding city in a voice that I knew. My Mom was on speaking terms with all of Chicagoland, and somehow the city became less threatening, even friendly.

Rereading that paragraph, I suddenly knew that my essay was not about my longing for fame, or my mother's role in the early days of television. It was about me, and one way that I found to overcome a suburban boy's fears of the big city. To use Barry's metaphor, my draft triggered a horse race of meaning, and an idea that was at first well-buried in the pack suddenly sprinted forward to surprise me.

One of the hardest things for me to learn about writing is that I don't have to get it right the first time. Drafts often have holes big enough for the wind to blow through. That's why I have a sign over my desk that says "It Doesn't Count," to remind me that every draft is like a single photograph of many that could be taken of the same subject.

Seeing past the weaknesses of my drafts also remains a struggle for me—as it is for many writers—but it is essential. Dwelling on my "bad" writing blinds me to the strengths, which I must build on in revision. My internal critic has a sharp eye for error, but I am now teaching it to celebrate what's good in my drafts, to celebrate those magic lines that reveal me to myself, and to find joy in the simple act of having written.

BB

Follow Through

Dig out your typewriter or word processor and type the draft from your journal. If you're like me, you'll see plenty in your draft that displeases you. As you're typing, though, make sure you notice things you like, including lines or passages that sound good to you. Look for any clues about meaning; is there a paragraph or sentence that hints at or proclaims the results of the horse race of meaning in your story or essay?

Resist the temptation to perform major surgery on your draft as you type it. Save that for tomorrow.

First Draft: A Name Up in City Lights

When I was six or seven, Mom took me to the Merchandise Mart to put in an occasional appearance on a TV show called "Today on the Farm." She was a regular on the program, along with a lanky man with short hair named Eddie Arnold. I was enlisted as the generic child, whenever one was needed.

Once, I stood in front of the false front of a farmhouse and mouthed Christmas carols with a small group of other children, while Styrofoam snow fell steadily from a large cylinder suspended from the ceiling of the studio. Another time I sat on a bale of hay and chewed thoughtfully on a grass stem while guest star Chet Atkins plucked away on his guitar.

Even then, I thought about the irony of an early morning farm show being broadcast from the dark heart of the city. It was an early lesson in the pretense of television, which at the time was still young and thriving in Chicago.

Few people believed that Carmelita Pope was not a stage name. My mom did have a stage name once. As Carla Dare, she starred in one full-length motion picture called "Citizen Saint," about Chicago's own Mother Cabrini, who was canonized by the Catholic Church for her work among the city's poor. To this day, I have been unable to find a copy or even a mention of the film, though mom has shown me impressive publicity shots of herself in prayerful poses, decked out in a nun's black robes.

This was early in her career, after she left her native Chicago to make it big as an actress in New York, where a stage name seemed appropriate, even necessary.

But after she married my father, then a reporter with the *Chicago Tribune*, she returned home and began her career as a "Chicago television personality." She also returned to her maiden name for stage work.

One of the first quiz shows on television was called "Down You Go," which began in New York but later landed at WMAQ-TV in Chicago. The host of the program was Bergan Evans, an erudite and thoughtful-looking fellow, who was a brilliant semanticist at Northwestern University. He is not the kind of host who would be chosen for today's TV quiz shows. In old photographs of the show he looks distinctly uncomfortable on the set, and his thick glasses and ill-fitting suits would qualify him, in the modern terminology, as a "nerd."

But he was a supremely logical choice for the program, since it was a word game, and by all accounts he was a deft host. Mom was a panelist on the show, along with my godmother Tony Gilman, and two other Chicago celebrities. They had to guess phrases sent in by viewers as they were revealed, letter by letter. A wrong guess lit an arrow which pointed to the floor in front of the errant panelist.

The show was a hit, and in the publicity Mom was described as beautiful and bright, the latter a term seldom used to describe women in the early fifties. When she became pregnant with me, she left the show temporarily. But when she triumphantly returned, she brought me along and on the air I was christened the "Down You Go" baby.

It was the first of many speechless appearances I put in with my mom in my elusive quest for stardom in those early days of Chicago television.

When "Down You Go" had run its course, first on WMAQ and later on WGN, Mom signed on to do live commercial breaks on the evening news, first with Alex Drier and later with Floyd Kalber. Clint Yule did the weather. Several nights a week she would take me along, driving Edens Expressway from our suburban Highland Park home to the Merchandise Mart where WMAQ had its studios.

It was on those drives that I first became conscious of the city. It was both a frightening and fascinating place to a seven-year-old who, until then, knew it as a place where my father used to try to beat cops to homicides for the *Tribune*, and where black people lived unhappily, and traffic jams and robberies were routine. It was a place where a suburban kid like me could get lost forever, and even Lassie would never pick up the scent.

But when I would watch from the darkened control booth as Mom became Carmelita Pope, spokesperson for Illinois Natural Gas Company or Bell Savings, live on the evening news with Alex Drier, I realized that she was talking directly to that dark and forbidding city, in a voice that I knew. My mom was on speaking terms with all of Chicagoland, and somehow the city became less threatening, even friendly.

I appeared with her several times on these ads, once again in the role of the speechless, generic child. I remember my most difficult assignment was to toss a baseball back and forth with my brother, while Mom praised the interest that could be earned with a modest deposit in a Bell Savings account.

There was some tension in the studio that night. The director was concerned that 1) we might drop the ball while on the air, and 2) we might throw it through one of the stage lights. Before the spot, we practiced endlessly, though I was quietly confident. Baseball was my specialty in those days, and I wasn't in the habit of fluffing easy lobs. I was more worried about my brother, who was something of a clod with a hardball.

It went well, and I was recruited for other ads now and then whenever a living prop in the six- to nine-year-old age group was needed.

My passion for baseball was boundless in those days. And when sportscaster Jack Brickhouse, whom Mom had gotten to know at WGN, invited all of us to join him in the broadcast booth at the Cub's Wrigley Field, I very nearly swooned with anticipation. We arrived early, and Mr. Brickhouse took us down to the dugout to meet some of the players and collect autographs on the program. I still have several framed photographs, taken by some generous team photographer, of my mom and my brother and me standing awkwardly with Ernie Banks and pitcher Dick Ellsworth—Banks in his famous batting stance, and Ellsworth staring at the stitching on a hardball. I seem frozen with awe.

The Cubs were playing the Los Angeles Dodgers that day, and Maury Wills was the reigning king of stolen bases. With little urging, he took us all to second base to demonstrate his technique, while thousands of Chicagoans in the stands looked on. At that moment, the city seemed to be mine. I was a celebrity, or rather, the son of one.

I was a little confused on that point until Jack Brickhouse finally took us up to the broadcast booth, which was suspended high over the grandstand behind home plate. I was always afraid of heights, and immediately found a corner in the booth where both shoulders would touch walls and cowered in fear. To have risen to such heights of delusion on the playing field only to fall apart one hundred feet above it was a sobering experience.

Mr. Brickhouse was kind and sympathetic, and suggested that we might be more comfortable in the box seats below. But before we descended, he mentioned between pitches that Carmelita Pope and her family had dropped by to say hello, and that made me feel better. I was the son of a celebrity again.

But things were never quite the same after that. I lost faith in my own eventual stardom, so that when Mom got us tickets to WGN's Bozo's Circus I refused to sit in the grandstand on stage and chose instead to sit out of camera range in the darkened auditorium seats, even though I would give up the chance to play the Grand Prize Game. For weeks before the program I had practiced for the event, tossing ping pong balls into metal buckets, and while my confidence grew in the accuracy of my arm, I lost faith in my ability to keep it together on camera. I developed stage fright.

Chicago television's move from live programming to video tape should have reassured me—if you blow it they can always do it over—but I began to spurn Mom's offers to join her when she taped ads or put in public appearances. Instead, I would take her old scripts and used cue cards (she called them "idiot cards"), and stage my own productions in the cool safety of the basement of my Highland Park home. But it was hopeless. I was beginning to believe in my inevitable anonymity again, and Chicago again became an alien place for me. Like most white suburban kids from up north, I restricted my movements to Michigan Avenue if I came to Chicago at all.

But as my star fell, Mom's continued to rise. She became national spokesperson for Pam, a spray-on vegetable spray that keeps things from sticking to pans, and for six years she appeared during commercial breaks across the country, holding the can close to her cheek and announcing her name.

In Chicago, the name Carmelita Pope rang a bell with many TV viewers, but she was something of a mystery to the rest of the nation. One night, I watched while Burt Reynolds strutted to his chair on Johnny Carson's Tonight Show, and his first one-liner was "Who the hell is Carmelita Pope, anyway?" Not long after that, someone showed me a copy of the membership card for the Carmelita Pope Fan Club, which had gotten started at Goddard College in Vermont. In addition to the usual blanks for the holder's name, there was a large graphic of two eggs flying off a frying pan.

None of this bothered Mom or me. What bothered me was the future of the ozone layer. I had forfeited my dream of stardom on Chicago television to become a passionate crusader for ecology, and worried that the freon contained in cans of Pam would pollute the atmosphere. Mom reminded me that the product helped pay for the college tuition that allowed me to know what the ozone layer was, and I said no more.

The fact was that I was always very proud of my mom. And when I finally gave up my own longing for celebrity, and even stopped feeling like the *son* of a Chicago celebrity, I was even prouder. Maybe it's an inevitable part of growing up, giving up some of the self-centeredness that distracts children from appreciating not only the accomplishments of their parents, but the great difficulty of making them happen.

Twelve years ago, when mom told me she was leaving Chicago television to move to Los Angeles, which had become TV's mecca, I realized the great risks involved for her. In a sense, she was starting in the business all over again, in a place where youth is a cult, and parts for older women are few.

Before she left Chicago for good, she did a few TV and radio spots for Magikist Carpets. The Magikist sign along Edens, with its red neon lips that hovered above the expressway and flashed messages to drivers, had always seemed a gateway to the city to me as I drove in from the north. Whenever I saw it, my grip on the steering wheel tightened as I readied myself to do battle on city streets.

When the house in Highland Park was sold, I drove away in a U-Haul truck with some furniture and artifacts from my earlier life, and headed south toward the city on my way to my Connecticut home. As I approached the Magikist sign, I hunkered down for the tension and traffic of the city ahead. On the message board below, I suddenly noticed the name "Carmelita Pope" sweep along the grid of white bulbs, and then it was gone.

I'm not sure what the message was—probably something about where to call for a cleaning special on shag carpets, or some slogan from the new ad campaign. It didn't matter. For a moment, I felt like I did when I would watch Mom from the control booth, talking live to the vast city from a cluttered studio in the Merchandise Mart. Chicago seemed friendlier, smaller. And it felt like I was leaving home.

Day Nineteen: Divorcing the Draft

Take the typewritten draft you finished yesterday (or any other draft you have around the house that you think deserves revision). Get a pair of scissors. Cut up the draft by paragraphs. (You might choose to keep some chunks of dialogue intact, but try to look for ways to cut it into smaller units.)

Shuffle your stack of paragraphs.

Now it's time to judge the horse race of meaning. Go through your paragraph pile and find what you think is the most important, or the "core" paragraph. If you're working on an essay or article, that might be the one that indicates your main point, or the paragraph that most reveals to you what you might be trying to say, like the one I found yesterday on page three of my draft. If you're writing a short story, it might be the paragraph with the key moment, scene, or situation that seems to have the most significance (see "Getting to the Heart of the Story," page 78).

It is sometimes hard to find this core; it may, in fact, be missing. For now, though, go out on a limb and choose one paragraph that seems to point to your purpose in the draft, that seems to come closest to the one thing it's *really* about. Set that core paragraph aside.

Now go through the stack of paragraphs that remain and scrutinize them like a drill sergeant. Set aside any that seem to have no relevance to the core, or don't further the dominant meaning of the draft. If part of a paragraph does seem important, cut away the irrelevant material. Save the purposeful lines, and set aside the rest.

This process is a little like stringing popcorn. First you hunt for the thread that might hold your essay or story together, then you carefully choose the kernels that belong on that thread. Try stringing your draft together in the same way.

On your writing desk, spread out the paragraphs you've saved — including your core paragraph — and play with order. Try new leads, new ends, new middles. Don't worry about the missing transitions. You can add those later. Don't worry about preserving the chronology of the original draft. Writers often manipulate time when it serves their purpose.

As you arrange and rearrange your essay, you may find a use for some of the paragraphs you thought were irrelevant. You might find that you can literally cut away words, lines, or passages that serve no purpose. Most of all, you might have ideas for new material that is missing: a scene, an observation, a bit of dialogue, some background information, a new character, another experience that you'd forgotten that suddenly seems to belong. With tape and paper, splice this new material into the draft as you rebuild it from the unshapely shreds that were once neat, typewritten pages.

Seeing What You Said

Was it hard to attack your typed draft with a pair of scissors? Did it seem somehow sacrilegious? Did a "core" paragraph emerge from the pack, or did everything seem equally important or equally unimportant?

Did you change your mind about what that core really was as you played with the fragments of your draft? Did you feel like throwing everything away and starting over? Did you end up with just a few paragraphs from the first draft, or did you end up reassembling it in pretty much the same way?

Writer to Writer

I used to love the way the carbon ribbon on my IBM Selectric typewriter made clean, crisp letters on the unblemished page. I loved the look of the page when I was done — all those neat black lines symmetrically arranged, all those words marching with military precision at my command. Though I was often dissatisfied with what those words said, I was not going to mess with that page. It just looked too good. The thought of taking a pencil to my typed manuscript and hacking away at the clutter, or writing in ideas for new material, or blocking out whole paragraphs, seemed a bit like marking up a favorite book. You just don't do that.

I later learned the need to disrespect the typewritten page, even to take satisfaction in plowing up those neat rows of words with a pencil when they didn't seem to serve any purpose. Now my drafts are a mess. (I learned to write in books, too.)

But it was hard to get used to. Somehow when the draft was typed, the words tended to harden into concrete. It seemed finished, despite its problems. Even worse, I sometimes became so close to the draft and what it said that I couldn't break with it when I needed to. It was a lot like a troubled love relationship; when you invest a lot of time and energy in the thing, you really don't want to admit that it's on the rocks.

A few years ago I spent six weeks laboring over an article about my father's alcoholism (for the final draft, see page 148). When I was done, the piece was fifteen manuscript pages long, and though the process of writing it led to a number of personal revelations, I slipped slowly into despair. I knew the article was not very good.

I was desperate. After all the time and work and personal pain involved in writing the piece, I wondered if anything could be salvaged to sell. I wondered if my failure to produce a quality manuscript after six weeks of trying meant I was a lousy writer. I wondered if I would ever understand my father enough to write about him well.

Somehow I found the will to attempt a revision. I went over the manuscript again and again, hunting down threads that could be followed, passages I liked, considering alternative designs. I fingered the pages until they were dog-eared. But as the revision began to emerge from my typewriter, my despair deepened. It wasn't much different from the first draft, and it wasn't much better.

Working on the revision became torture, and finally it became clear to me that I had to stop, so I set it aside.

Later, I realized the problem was not that my subject was too difficult, or my writer's will too weak. The problem was that my revision was not a revision. I was unable to move from that initial vision of my subject, as I had done when I took multiple photographs of the old elm tree with my camera. For all its flaws, I was in love with my first draft and couldn't bring myself to file for divorce.

There are ways to break out of this tight relationship with a draft in need of revision. Perhaps the best medicine is time. My frustration with the piece on my father seemed to offer no other alternative, so I put it away for another six months. When I opened that drawer again, it was finally possible for me to read the manuscript with enough detachment to even smile at its flaws. I knew then that the affair was over. I could let it go. This exercise suggests two other ways that make it easier to break with the draft:

- *Write it fast.* Yesterday I urged you to spend no more than a day or two writing your way to the end of your first draft. The longer we toil over it, the more likely we are to fall into its grip. For all its flaws, a fast draft can have a spontaneity and freshness that is missing from a carefully constructed one. And partly because of its obvious weaknesses, it's easier to revise.

- *Attack it physically.* The first time I attempted this cut-and-paste method of revision, it seemed heretical to take a pair of scissors and chop my carefully composed prose into pieces. I was still hung up on the sanctity of the typed page. But once it was disassembled, I was able to forget how tight I was with the draft — it was gone — and it was much easier to focus on the pieces that showed promise. If I had known to take scissors to the draft on my father's alcoholism, I might have more quickly found a way to make it better.

Cutting up yesterday's draft transformed the piece (see the cut-and-paste revision on pages 75-77). I cut away nearly six pages of material that no longer seemed to further my meaning. After I discovered that my essay was really about how my mother's TV career altered my relationship with Chicago, I was able to see that my anecdotes about baseball, Bozo's circus, my mom's role in the quiz show, and my own longing to be a celebrity no longer belonged.

I also discovered a drastically different order for the remaining material. For example, the fourteenth paragraph in the original draft now comes third in the revision. The fourth paragraph in the revision used to be the twenty-fourth in the draft, and so on. The piece still has problems (before I begin the third draft, I need to do more freewriting), but it's much more focused and much more tightly organized.

The hardest thing about revision is throwing good stuff away. I really liked some of the material in my reject pile. But this method makes it easier for me to see what really belongs and what doesn't. Like spurning a lover, there is still some pain involved in letting go. But from the wreckage of the first draft, a new essay emerges that is more satisfying, more whole, and more willing to share its meaning with me and my readers.

BB

A Voice That I Knew

When I was six or seven, ~~Mom~~ [my mother] took me to ~~the~~ [Chicago's] Merchandise Mart
to put in an occassional appearance on a TV show called "Today on
the Farm." She was a regular on the program, along with a lanky [young, and]
~~and wholesome-looking singer~~ ~~fellow with short hair~~ named Eddie Arnold. I was enlisted as the
generic child, whenever one was needed.

Even then, I thought about the irony of an early morning
farm show being broadcast from the dark heart of the city.

It was a city I remember mostly in the light of ~~early~~ [late]
[afternoon] ~~evening~~, looking through the car window as Mom [, Carmelita Pope,] drove in from our
suburban [Highland Park] home to do the live commercial breaks on WMAQ's ~~evening~~ [6 o'clock]
news, first with Alex Drier, and later with Floyd Kalber.
audience: will non-Chicagoans know these people? does it matter?

I appeared with her several times on these ads, once again
in the role of the speechless, generic child. I remember my most
difficult assignment was to toss a baseball back and forth with
my brother, while Mom praised the interest that could be earned
with a modest deposit in a Bell Savings account.

In Chicago, the name Carmelita Pope rang a bell with many TV
viewers, but she was something of a mystery to the rest of the
nation. One night, [many years later] I watched ~~while~~ Burt Reynolds strutted to his
chair on Johnny Carson's "Tonight Show", and his first one-liner
was "Who the hell is Carmelita Pope, anyway?" Not long after
that, someone showed me a copy of the membership card for the
Carmelita Pope Fan Club, which had gotten started at Goddard

APD

14

24

Need to freewrite more about this. What exactly did that city look like to me through the car window? What else do I remember about the city back then?! Need more information.

College in Vermont. In addition to the usual blanks for the
holder's name, there was a large graphic of two eggs flying off a
frying pan.

*After two decades as a "Chicago television personality," Mom found her way
into the homes of television watchers across the country, as the*
national spokesperson for Pam, a spray-on vegetable spray that
keeps things from sticking to pans, ~~and~~ for six years she
appeared during commericial breaks across the country, holding
the can close to her cheek and announcing her name.

*Could have
more fun
with this
Pam stuff*

23

But it was in Chicago, in the fifties and early sixties,
where I will always see my mother's celebrity most clearly. It
was then I was most touched by it. It was also a time when the
boundaries of my safe suburban world suddenly expanded to include
the city—an alien, frightening place that until then I knew
mostly through the dark stories my father would tell about
covering homicides as a reporter for the <u>Tribune.</u>

*Add more
information
here. Freewrite
about my father's
stories?*

ADD

But when I would watch from the darkened control booth as
Mom became Carmelita Pope, spokesperson for Illinios Natural Gas
Company or Bell Savings, live on the evening news with Alex
Drier, I realized that she was talking directly to that dark and
forebidding city, in a voice that I knew. My Mom was on speaking
terms with all of Chicagoland, and somehow the city became less
threatening, even friendly.

13

Twelve years ago, when Mom told me she was leaving Chicago
television to move to Los Angeles, which had become TV's mecca, I
realized the great risks that involved for her. In a sense, she
was starting in the business all over again, in a place where
youth is ~~a cult~~ *worshipped*, and parts for older women are few.

2⁷

Before she left Chicago for good, she did a few TV and radio spots for Magikist Carpets. The Magikist sign along Edens, with

its red neon lips that hovered above the expressway and flashed messages to drivers, had always seemed a gateway to the city to me as I drove in from the north. Whenever I saw it, my grip on the steering wheel tightened as I readied myself to do battle on city streets.

When the house in Highland Park was sold, I drove away in a U-Haul truck with some furniture and other artifacts from my earlier life, and headed south toward the city on my way to my Connecticut home. As I approached the Magikist sign, I hunkered down for the tension and traffic of the city ahead. On the message board below, I suddenly noticed the name "Carmelita Pope" sweep along the grid of white bulbs, and then it was gone.

I'm not sure what the message was—probably something about where to call for a cleaning special on shag carpets, or some slogan from the new ad campaign. It didn't matter. For a moment I felt like I did when I would watch Mom from the control booth, talking live to the vast city from a cluttered studio in the Merchandise Mart. Chicago seemed friendlier, smaller. And it felt like I was leaving home.

Next draft needs more information about why the city seemed such a forbidding place. Lost the richness of detail of earlier draft.

Follow Through

When you're finished cutting away what is no longer important, splicing in new material, and playing with the order of your story or essay, tape it all together. Then retype the revision.

Compare the revision with the draft. Is it stronger? Spend three minutes freewriting, beginning with this phrase: "The hardest thing about revision for me is . . ."

Getting to the Heart of the Story

Short story writer Andre Dubus says that a novel is about an entire world but a short story is about one thing. When I slice apart the draft of a short story, I look for that one thing on which the story centers itself. It is usually an incident, a significant moment where a character realizes something for the first time, or maybe fails to realize something. Sometimes the most significant moment doesn't even occur in the story. For example, Grandmother is dead and the story is about the reverberations of that death on the surviving family. But somewhere in that story, a character will begin to learn something or to change. This is what I look for.

For Day Nineteen, I sliced apart an old story called "Elijah in Amsterdam." It is a science fiction story about a time traveler from the twenty-first century who goes back to rescue Anne Frank from the Nazis. The story began for me when I visited the Anne Frank Museum in Amsterdam. I felt enormously protective toward Anne, and as I stood among the crowds of tourists, I couldn't help feeling that nobody really understood her. This place had become a shrine to sentimentality instead of a monument to a wonderful young woman and a fine writer who grew up in a time when Europe was a mess. I had this overwhelming urge to go back there and talk to her, to show her the translations of her diary and show her the power and meaning of her nightly scribbling, to make her understand that she didn't die in vain.

I worked hard on "Elijah in Amsterdam" but it never really came alive, partly due to the story's ambition and partly to its lack of direction. When I hacked it up and shuffled the paragraphs, one of them jumped out at me. It was after Claude, the main character, kidnaps Anne Frank and brings her to the Anne Frank Museum forty years later. He shows her the different translations of her diary and tries to stop her from looking at the photo exhibit which tells of the Nazi atrocities. He hugs her as though this one hug could change the course of history. She knees him in the groin and rushes away into the crowd.

This is the core of the story. Claude's sentimental paternal feelings toward Anne are not returned. Anne knows she must go back to 1944 because her death will have more impact on the world than any other books she could write in her life. But the story is about Claude and how he finds out he can't rescue the helpless Anne, because she isn't helpless. You see, my feelings in that museum toward Anne were just as sentimental as those of the tourists I had criticized. I didn't realize this until I wrote two drafts of this story. You learn things when you write, and they are not always the things you expect to learn.

I need to develop his character more in a revision so the reader can understand his failure. He needs more of a motive for kidnapping Anne. Maybe he has a daughter who died in a future war or was taken from him in the divorce court. Maybe he is a history buff out to cure all the injustices of Time. Maybe he is a Jewish man in search of his cultural identity.

Already I see other paragraphs that don't fit, information that just isn't necessary because it's not connected with the core. For example, I spend a lot of time in the first draft describing the time travel center and Claude's home. I can gloss over a lot of this material now that I know where the story's energy lies.

This needs to be a simple story about a man who tries to change history but fails, and ultimately it's a story about how the real Anne Frank is much more powerful, beautiful, and independent than any one person's feelings about her.

Finding the core helps me to see.

BL

Day Twenty:
The Myth of the Boring Story

Maybe you like what you've written, or maybe you'd like to line the nearest gerbil cage with it, or maybe you have no idea what to think of it. Maybe you are bored stiff with the original idea. Maybe you feel all four. If that's the case, then you're probably well on your way to becoming a writer.

Put your draft aside. Hide it in a drawer. Bury it under your mattress or in the glove compartment of your car. Don't look at it. Take a break.

Think of a story you and everybody else knows well, a fairy tale that was told to you over and over in childhood, such as "The Three Little Pigs" or "Rapunzel." How could you retell it to enliven the reader's interest? One way would be to write the story from a different point of view. For example: How many points of view are there in "The Three Little Pigs"? You could say four—the three pigs and the wolf. But what about the wolf's psychologist and the third pig's stockbroker? What about Barbara Walters and Paul Harvey? Now that you get the idea, pick a fairy tale and write it from a different angle. Write quickly and don't forget to enjoy yourself.

Seeing What You Said

What information did you leave out of the original story? What new insight does your point of view give to the story?

Was it easy to retell the story or did you find your enthusiasm lagging halfway through?

When you look at your new version, what new information does the reader learn about the original story?

Writer to Writer

A few summers ago, I was inspired by a book written by a German scholar. The book proved the Brothers Grimm were frauds, that they did not collect folk tales from the Bavarian forest but made them up. The author's proof rested on several strong points of evidence, including the different published versions of the fairy tales themselves as they've gone through revisions. It was striking how much better the tales grew through the different editions, and the author speculated that these were more a result of Jacob Grimm's pen than any research the brothers had done. I decided if Jacob Grimm made up his fairy tales I could rewrite a few of them as folk songs.

I started with the story of the three little pigs. My first dismal attempt began something like,

> *"Three little pigs*
> *building a house.*
> *Three little pigs,*
> *East, north and south.*

> *First little pig thought*
> *straw was the best.*
> *Second little pig*
> *used sticks for his nest.*

I was bored stiff with the idea. I sounded like Captain Kangaroo on a bad day. There were too many familiar versions of the story running through my head. I needed to reconnect imaginatively with the subject so I could discard the boring information and focus on the new stuff. But I couldn't do it without rethinking the story.

Then I thought of switching the point of view to that of the big bad wolf and I wrote one stanza, which led to another and another.

There's nothing wrong with a big bad wolf, is there?
I mean, isn't a big bad wolf just about the same as a furry bear?
So forget about those three little hogs over there
and listen to the song that I sing.

(chorus)
I love pigs' eyes
I love pigs' ears
I love pork chow mein.

I love pigs' tongue
I love pigs' blood
Pig toes drive me insane.

I'm just a big bad wolf
who hasn't got a name.
So don't be surprised
when I eat you.

First little pig, he's got a house of straw.
They taste real good over an open flame,
but they're much better raw.

So I huffed and I puffed
and I blew the whole thing to Saginaw,
and the sweet little fella turned to me and this is what I said,

(chorus)

Second little pig,
he's got a house of wood.
A little mustard, or some mayonnaise,
that would be good.

Y'know all this huffin' and puffin's got me feelin' like I should
have a little more somethin' to eat.
So I tell him,

(chorus)

Those two little pigs got up my appetite.
One more and I think I'll call it a night.
But the house is made of brick
so I slide down the chimney quick,
but I land in a pot of boiling water,
and the little pig turns to me (and he talks like Peter Lorre or Bob Dylan)
and he says:

(Final chorus)
I love wolf eyes
I love wolf ears
I love wolf chow mein.

I love wolf tongue
I love wolf blood
Wolf toes drive me insane.
I'm just a little pig
who hasn't got a name
so don't be surprised when I eat you.

The song was fun to write and I think it adds a new dimension to the original story. Like Bruce's revision of his essay, I discarded a lot of the original information once I found a tighter focus. The wolf's view of things gives the listener a new way of interpreting the story. The meaning is no longer, "If you build your house strong enough, the wolf won't get you," but more like, "Animals with no names tend to eat other animals with no names."

I didn't intend to write a song with this cruel meaning, but when I think about it now I realize I am reacting to all the cute versions of the story I was told in childhood. Pigs don't wear plaid sportcoats or play the fiddle or dance. At a certain level I resent these frolicking Walt Disney pigs. I get a sick feeling in my stomach, like when I visited a Victorian museum in England and saw a display of stuffed guinea pigs in tuxedos and bowler hats drinking tea. The wolf is an animal and his voice helps put the story in animal terms. As soon as he began to speak, the song wrote itself.

I wish I could say the same for the draft I tried to write yesterday at Bruce's bidding (see page 85). I have a confession to make. I couldn't finish it. I wrote two pages and ran out of gas. I got bored and all my demons of doubt came to torment me. "What do you want to write about a dead woman for?" they say. "It's a clever idea, but you'll never pull it off." Or, "The trouble with this story is that it's not real. Write about what you know. You don't know anything about what it's like to be dead, let alone what it's like to be a woman. You are a phony. Look at Bruce, at least he is writing about something he knows about. Why don't you write about *your* mother?" And so on and so on.

These voices are not unusual, and though they sound harsh, I don't ignore them, but simply look beyond them to things I like in the manuscript. I like the scene in the supermarket where she reads the soap labels. I've always been taken by the religious names companies give to detergent. I like my description of how it feels to be floating in time without a body. I like how I'm starting to learn a bit more about this woman, how her husband Tom is not as close to her as I had originally imagined, and how she has grown-up children (originally I thought she was a younger woman but now I know she is in her fifties). I like how I'm supposed to be making up this story, but everything I write I've seen or heard before. The white colonial house is the house I was born in. The red polka-dotted cotton dress is one my mother had when she was younger, and that whole sequence on the porch comes straight out of an eight-millimeter home movie that sits in the cellar of my parents' house in Dover, New Hampshire. Fiction writers don't make things up, they just rearrange.

What I like best about this story is its ambition. I'm trying to figure something out about death, a subject I think most people think about often but never try to tackle in a story.

As I write, memories flash before me. My mother sees her mother standing in her bedroom doorway the morning of her death. She calls out, and my mother wakes up. Two hundred miles away in New York City, my grandmother dies. In Isaac Bashevis Singer's novel, *The Slave*, a young woman comes back from the dead to find her lover. In a news story I once read in the *New York Times Magazine*, a little girl, who fell into a well and hovered on the brink of death for months, comes to her mother and tells her to stop praying, she wants to go.

A student in my freshman English class wrote about a similar experience. Her grandmother returned from the dead to reach out from her bedroom closet and tell her it was OK. And two Halloweens ago, my friend John Rule told how disturbed he was as a young boy when his grandfather died. Then he had a dream. His grandfather stood in front of him and poked at his stomach, tickling him. His grandfather smiled at him and seemed happier than he'd ever known him to be. I remember how John turned to the people at the Halloween party, his bearded face flickering in the candlelight, and said, "I never felt sad about my grandfather's death after that dream."

The more I talk about this story, the more I realize I have to write it, if only to discover why I am writing it. My demons of doubt come from a lack of definite direction, a fear that this woman will just dissolve in smoke. It's not uncommon for me to get stuck this way. In fact, I could say it's part of my process. I need to let the story stew a little more inside me before I write the draft. It's comforting to know that other writers share my queasy process. Norman Mailer says, "When I'm in the middle of a novel I feel like a monk in the wrong monastery."

I need to find the right monastery. To reconnect with my original excitement for this story and redefine it the way I did with the fairy tale and the way Bruce did when he found the emerging meaning in his draft.

There are no boring stories, only boring storytellers.

BL

Follow Through

Take a few minutes and think about the most boring story you can imagine, a story like, "I went to the laundromat, did my laundry and came home." Write your one paragraph story at the top of a blank page.

Now, compose a new story about the same subject that is not boring. You may wish to change the point of view, or maybe just describe the laundromat in an unusual way. Take the time to write a few leads before you begin. Circle your subject to find the right angle.

Here are a few tips to help keep you working when you feel bored with your writing.

Work on something new. Part of boredom with material comes from overexposure. Starting new things helps to keep ideas popping in the old things you're working on.

Spend a few minutes a day freewriting about your piece. Write about your feelings toward it and how they've changed. Try to get a picture of how the piece is developing or not developing. Label your boredom and you may begin to see how to relabel your excitement.

Go for walks, play tennis, swim, run, go to a movie, read. Do anything but write for a day or two. Think about your piece as a difficult mathematical problem you are musing about. Don't allow yourself to indulge in negativity.

Though you may never find the answer, you must never lose sight of the question.

Realize that writing is a roller coaster. If you are down, you will go up. And the higher you go up, the faster you come down. Don't be discouraged when your enthusiasm comes down too low. Don't get too excited when you go up too high. Pace yourself.

THE LAST DAY
Unfinished draft

She was on her way to the supermarket, but suddenly she had no car, no fingers gripping the steering wheel, no legs and arms, no shopping list. She slipped through the glass doors and floated like smoke up and down the aisles. She had never noticed how beautiful the cans and jars were stacked so neatly on the shelves, how green was the cellophane grass where the bananas sat heaped in a pile, how the bags of flour puffed out their little chests so proudly. And the people in the supermarket. She could see inside them. She could float past the carts full of beer and Wonderbread into their eyes. It was like stepping through the hard crust of snow to the soft powder beneath or opening a black door and being bathed in warm orange light. That old man who looks so sad, whose eyes are storm shutters, the years stretched like old rags over his cheekbones. Look inside and see the young boy running in the summer breeze, a child washed in the clear light of his mother's smile. His breath sweet as candy. His voice a morning lark. They were all prisoners in these bodies, she thought, like the groceries trapped in the clanging steel cages or the food stuffed into the gleaming packages.

She was in the soap aisle when she realized she hadn't bought anything. She couldn't because she was no longer alive. Dead was the proper term. That word like a hoofbeat pounding on the joy which swelled in her. For a moment she saw the truck swerve into her path. She heard the screech of the tires, the shattering glass, the sirens wailing like lost souls calling her. Then the rising feeling like a large bird spreading its wings inside her chest. What does it mean to die? She had spent most of her life trying to figure out what it meant to be alive.

She looked at the row of detergents. She read the names slowly one at a time— "JOY, DAWN, AWAKE, YES, CHEER, TIDE, WISK." She read them as though they were prayers which anchored her to this place. If she stopped reading them, she would fly away like a helium balloon on a wave of Muzak to some place far beyond where nothing would be familiar. "ARISE, ALL, TONE, DIAL, IVORY, EPIC, SUN." She could feel herself going, the supermarket shrinking to the size of a gumdrop on the blacktop beneath. She was going to him. He was calling her.

Like a melody she swept down through the pitched roof of their house on Fairview Avenue. She rolled along the walls and curled herself around the sofa and the coffee table full of souvenir ashtrays they had gotten on their trips together. He was upstairs, sitting on the end of the bed, with the telephone in his hand. The telephone was beeping and a strange mechanical voice was saying, "IF YOU WISH TO MAKE A CALL, PLEASE HANG UP AND DIAL AGAIN OR PHONE THE OPERATOR FOR DIRECTORY ASSISTANCE." His face was pale and his eyes were red. His shirt was wrinkled and his hair was sticking up in different directions. She stood beside him and felt the tug of his grief like an ocean tide pulling her out into the infinite.

"Claire," he said. "Don't leave me Claire, please."

"I haven't gone," she said. "I'm here."

He could not hear her, nor could he feel it when she wrapped herself around his chest. He was sitting on the bed, he was drowning.

"Please," she said. "Don't mourn me. I'm happy, happier than I've ever been."

"I never showed you how much I loved you. I didn't know how."

"Stop being so melodramatic. You'll die too. You can show me then."

She stood in front of him and looked into his eyes. He was Tom, the man she had lived with all those years, the man whose shirts she'd washed. The man who had helped raise their children. She could never see too deeply into those eyes. There was always something that stopped her, like a wall of lead that closed like a portcullis. Now she could see in there but she didn't want to look, something held her back, a sense of modesty, perhaps, or was it was fear?

She left him sitting there, the phone still in his hand. She took one last look at the bedroom, beds she had forgot to make, the clothes on the floor she had forgot to bring downstairs, the shoes she had forgot to stick on the rack in the closet. She overcame the urge to put things in order, the sense of embarrassment that people would see her house this way. She melted like butter through the ceiling and drifted into the sky.

It was a feeling of lightness, like being a bubble that could never pop but just drifted here and there in the wind, except it wasn't wind at all but something else you couldn't feel, but was full of strength and direction, like a thousand voices chanting one steady melody in a low throbbing tone that grew stronger and stronger.

She looked down, and there was the old colonial house with the black shutters. It was summer and the clothesline was full of white sheets. She stood on the gray porch beside her mother, and watched herself sleep as a baby in the bassinet. There were squirrels in the trees chasing branches across the sky, and the sun was beating down on her mother's freckled face.

"I love you, Claire," her mother whispered as she picked the baby up and lifted her to her shoulder against the white cotton dress with the red polka dots.

The image began to flicker like a movie caught in a defective projector. The sun washed away the house and the summer and once again she was drifting.

Day Twenty-One:
The Myth of the Boring Storyteller or The William F. Buckley Shoe Shuffle

Think of a very sophisticated person, the kind of person you would be shocked to see in a bathroom. Think of William F. Buckley, Jr. or Queen Elizabeth or Prince Charles. Now, pretend you are this person writing a letter to a friend, describing an incident that happened this afternoon. You stepped in a pile of dog dung.

Freewrite for ten minutes. Begin.

Now, think of a less cultured person, someone like a New York cab driver — the kind of person who doesn't mince their words, if ya' know what I mean. This person is writing a letter to their friend describing what they saw this afternoon (the fella from the first part stepping in the poop).

Freewrite for another ten minutes. Begin.

Seeing What You Said

Did you find yourself struggling to write in a different voice, or was it easy?

Which part of the exercise did you have the most fun writing? Why?

Of the two people, which is closer to your written voice? What is the difference in how each of these characters describes the doggy by-product?

Writer to Writer

In school I was taught to write like the person in the first part of this exercise. He uses big words like "organic canine rubble," not because his subject is complex, but because he likes to distance himself from the world and display his prodigious vocabulary. Unwitting school teachers still promote this attitude with vocabulary quizzes which give students the feeling that their *own* words, acquired through reading and speech, are somehow inadequate.

I am always saddened at how many students tell me at the beginning of a writing course, "I will be a good writer as soon as I get a bigger vocabulary."

I can still remember the days when I used to write poetry using Roget's Thesaurus. They were silly, abstract poems with images like "sonorous azure waves" and "gleaming anathemas." These poems always felt incomplete, mainly because I didn't know what the heck they meant. None of the words were *my* words; therefore, they weren't *live* words. Live words are the ones we know, the ones which sprout meaning through appearances in our speech and in our reading. Dead words belong to someone else, usually a dictionary or William F. Buckley (they're not dead for him because he knows them). They create unnecessary space between author and subject (for more on dead words, see Day Thirty-Two).

I'm not suggesting that we always write like a cab driver, only that we understand that his honest, unflinching approach to a subject is a quality all good writing shares.

Our written voices develop the more we forget them. When we stop trying to impress others, we naturally begin wrestling with what we have to say. As young writers, we need room to discover these written voices just as we did our spoken ones in infancy.

A few years ago, I was involved in an elaborate deception which helped to teach me something about voice and writing. I began to write a column for a newspaper under the name of Renee Newman, a woman. The first one was called the Orgasm Indicators and was a comic commentary on a news story I heard on the radio about how monogamous women had more orgasms than swinging singles. It was well-received, so I wrote more, using my women friends as resources whenever I got stuck on a particularly important piece of research. In two years I wrote over twenty columns as Renee. The editor—who didn't know my real identity—sent me encouraging letters saying how much she enjoyed my stuff and would I like to come in and discuss working on larger pieces. I wrote her polite replies telling her how busy I was.

Finally, I decided I'd had enough of the deception and put Renee into retirement. I wrote a few humorous columns under my own name and all were rejected. "Your voice is contrived and somewhat predictable," one of the slips said. "You need to learn how to write in your own voice and not put on airs," another said.

One afternoon the phone rang, and it was the editor. She had called to tell me she was returning the three columns I had sent her that week in a final blitz. She didn't think they were funny. She didn't think I needed to send her anymore. Before the conversation ended, I let it slip that I knew Renee Newman. "YOU KNOW RENEE NEWMAN!" she shouted. "Where is she? She was the best writer we've ever had. I've been trying to find out where she is."

"She's been traveling in Africa, I think. Egypt, last I heard. She's coming home soon."

"Well, if you ever get in touch with her, tell her to send us stuff. We miss her."

"Fine. I'll tell her."

When she hung up I got a strange feeling. In one uncomfortable moment, I realized I was jealous of Renee Newman, my own creation. She could write about her life so candidly, and I was a sniveling wimp in comparison. I felt like Dustin Hoffman at the end of the movie *Tootsie*, after he's revealed his true identity to Jessica Lange and tells her, "I was more a man with you as a woman than I ever was as a man with any woman."

We all have different voices inside us, and writing is a way of unlocking them. I didn't have to be jealous of Renee Newman, because Renee Newman was as much a part of me as what I considered my own voice. Indeed, writing as Renee I was able to liberate that part of my written voice which confined itself to who I thought I was, or wanted to be. Young writers, like young people, often get preconceived ideas about who they are. Changing voices is a way of becoming more conscious of the range of possibility you possess as a writer. Only through experimentation do we begin to unravel our true voices and realize our true limitations.

Read your writing out loud and listen to your voice. If it bores you, maybe you're limiting your range as a writer. Do some of the follow-through exercises. Loosen up your ears. Start listening to some of the voices which sleep inside you.

BL

Follow Through

Freewrite for ten minutes:
- in the voice of your father or mother, describing you.
- in the voice of yourself as a very young child describing one of your parents.
- in the voice of a monster that haunted your childhood.
- in the voice of a member of the opposite sex forty years older than you.
- in the voice of a foreigner describing Americans.
- in the voice of a martian describing a bowling alley.

Day Twenty-Two:
Humor Is a Frog

You don't have to step on dog droppings to find a situation with comic potential. There is material everywhere, including (and perhaps especially) the newspaper. Read this, and you'll see what I mean:

Boston Globe
Sex segregation to eliminate fights at R.I. school ends with a treaty
Associated Press
WARWICK, R.I.—Segregation by sex on a school playground to protect boys
from the well-aimed kicks and punches of girls might be ending with a treaty that
follows a crush of nationwide publicity.
Principal Richard Sousa agreed Friday to allow the boys and girls of Oakland
Beach Elementary School to play together again on a trial basis beginning next
week to see if they will end their warring ways, students said.
The 430-pupil school drew national attention Friday when news of the reasons
for the segregation were reported in a local newspaper.
Boys complained they were being "kicked where it counts" by girls when they
went outside during recess periods. Sousa said the boy-girl fights were going on
almost daily since the school year began.
The agreement followed a meeting between a Sousa-appointed committee of
fifth- and sixth-grade boys and girls.
"He left us alone for 15 minutes or so to work on solutions on how we thought
we could solve the problem," said sixth-grader Leslie Fudge.
Under the agreement, the schoolyard will be united beginning Tuesday, but
will be segregated again if fighting resumes. If that happens, Sousa told the students he would agree to set aside a small portion of the playground for peaceful
mingling of boys and girls, Fudge said.
During an interview Friday, the principal said his aim was to have students
solve the problem "in an educational sort of way" so it would be a learning
experience.
© The Associated Press

Spend twenty minutes or so composing a humorous passage in your journal
based on this article, or go through today's paper and find one of your own.
Be playful. For example, try telling some part of the story that was untold in

the article (what *were* the negotiations like between the warring boys and girls?). Write about some character in the story you can imagine interviewing (who is the *real* Leslie Fudge?). Try speculating about what really happened, or what will happen next, or what could happen if things really get out of hand (a boys' rights movement taking shape in the schoolyard?). Or try exploring in a light-hearted way some experience you've had or observation you've made that relates to the events in the article. Most important, have fun. Begin.

Seeing What You Said

Were you able to easily find a humorous angle on your news clip, or did the humor seem forced and awkward?

Writer to Writer

I was always afraid to write humor because I thought the only thing worse than a serious writer who writes badly about serious things was a serious writer who tries to be funny and fails. I guess I still feel that way to some extent because I had to force myself to do this workout, especially after I decided that whatever I wrote would go in the book. I could hear my Watcher snickering in the background—"Write something humorous? You? Go ahead and embarrass yourself if you must. But I can't watch." I took my advice and plunged in:

> When boys and girls on a Rhode Island schoolyard recently penned a treaty to end their warring ways, principal Philip Sousa declared he hoped it would be a learning experience.
>
> "I learned how to bring a boy to his knees," said Leslie Fudge, sixth-grader and leader of a group of girls who allegedly kicked boys "where it counts" on the schoolyard. "I feel this will be extremely beneficial to me later in life. It's a man's world and I'm quite small and I'll need to see men eye to eye if I'm ever going to get ahead."
>
> Fabian Bloom, spokesperson for the boys, agreed that the experience, though painful, was educational. "We discussed it in biology class," he said. "Our teacher told us that most animals are equipped to feel pain because it helps them survive. I was glad to hear that. It explains a lot."
>
> Principal Sousa was relieved that the conflict between the boys and girls seems to have ended with a truce, but expressed concern that there would be lingering "pyschic trauma," especially among the boys. "Some have adjusted well," he said, "but others seem to be having trouble. We have several boys who say they're not sure they'll ever be able to make a commitment to a relationship after this experience."

"We've started a group to get them to talk about their feelings," Sousa said. "It's very well-attended."

School pyschologist Miranda Mathews says the girls seem much less affected by the incidents. "The only thing I've noticed among the girls recently is a keen interest in Tae Kwon Do."

Of course, it was much less difficult than I thought it would be, though my short composition isn't really very funny. But I enjoyed writing it. What I like best is that beneath the silliness, I think I'm starting to say something about the power of physical superiority, and what happens to some men when they lose it. I'm beginning to suggest that it might be a good thing. When I started writing this passage, I had no idea that it would take that turn, but I like it.

I could write a serious essay on the same angle, but I have a feeling it wouldn't be as good. That's not to say that humorists aren't serious writers. They are. "[Humorists] are not just fooling around," William Zinsser said in his classic *On Writing Well*.

They are as serious in purpose as Hemingway or Faulkner—in fact, a national asset in forcing the country to see itself clearly. To them humor is urgent work. It's an attempt to say important things in a special way that regular writers aren't getting said in a regular way—or, if they are, it's so regular that nobody is reading it.

Humorists like Art Buchwald, Erma Bombeck, Russell Baker, Nora Ephron, or Woody Allen are, of course, all keen observers of American culture. They pay attention to things not only for their comic potential, but for the same reason all writers do—because they feel strongly about them.

Sharing my writing, particularly writing I feel strongly about, is like dancing on the table in a crowded restaurant. It is a self-conscious act. Sharing my humor writing here is even more frightening. This time I dance away with no clothes on; I feel even more vulnerable, because I'm convinced I'm not nearly as funny as Barry (see "Infernal Combustion" page 97 if you want to see how funny he can be), and I've never really trusted my sense of humor.

But the self-doubts many of us feel about bringing our humor to the page are just another of our self-critic's ploys to stop us from taking risks. Don't be disappointed if your journal entry, like mine, seems unlikely to crack a smile, or might even be downright stupid. Don't try to analyze why your attempts sometimes seem to fall flat. "Humor can be dissected, as a frog can," wrote essayist E.B. White, "but the thing dies in the process." Just laugh at yourself and try again.

BB

Follow Through

Start a humor file. Clip newspaper articles that make you smile and shake your head and say to yourself, "Gosh, what a crazy world we live in." Paste them into your journal. Repeat this exercise when you're looking for something to experiment with.

You'd be amazed at how much topical material you can find in the paper with comic potential. In my file I've got an article about a cardboard cop that sits in a patrol car and intimidates drivers in Marlborough, New Hampshire. A creation of the police chief's wife, Marlene, "Captain Cardboard" sports glasses and a neatly trimmed moustache. "She cut it out, we put it in the cruiser, and God it works good," said the chief. She must have cut a fine figure, I thought.

Day Twenty-Three:
Me and the Tramp

Make a list of things that oppress you. Maybe you feel like you're in a minority. Maybe your height bothers you, you have no mechanical ability, or you could never roll your tongue. Maybe your big brother stole the ice cream cone you purposely ate slower so it would last. Maybe you have nightmares about the police coming to arrest you for all the times you tore the DO NOT REMOVE UNDER PENALTY OF LAW labels from pillows.

If you can't think of anything that oppresses you, think of things that bug or annoy you. It's the same thing. Make your list long, then pick one subject and freewrite about it for ten minutes.

Seeing What You Said

Was it easy to write about the subject? Did it bring back memories, or did it seem contrived?

When you read it out loud is it funny? Why? Why not? Do you think other people can identify with your problem?

Writer to Writer

The Swiss border at Geneva was a drive-through affair. A French Gendarme in a regal blue suit and white gloves stood in the glass building and waved through the approaching cars with a backhanded flip of his wrist and a somber nod. I was walking. I hadn't had a bath in weeks and all my clothes were soiled and stained with French pastry. The guard was short and he had big brass buttons on his jacket and a tiny automatic pistol stuck onto his hip. He told me to follow him and I did. We walked downstairs to the end of a long white corridor. There was a door, and he opened it and told me to step in. It was a closet with gray walls and a sour soap smell.

"Pull your pants down," he said in French, motioning with his hands about his belt.

"What?" I asked, a little stunned by his request.

"Pull your pants down!"

I undid the belt slowly and pulled them down to my knees and turned to him. He nodded and I pulled them up. I followed him back upstairs. My backpack had been completely emptied and all the belongings strewn along a big table. There was a jumbled mass of underwear, film, a camera, letters, dirty socks and crushed fruit. "You can go now," he said and began chatting with another guard who had left his post by the window several feet away from me. They chuckled together.

I stuffed a few belongings back in the pack. Out of the corner of my eye I saw a white Fiat approaching. My heart began to pound as I stepped in front of the window. With a delicate backhanded flick of the wrist I waved the car through and watched its beady taillights fade away into Switzerland. I looked over at the guards and they were still talking. Another car approached and I waved it through, then another, and another. With each flick of my wrist I could feel my humiliation slowly melting away.

There have been only a few times in my life when I felt like Charlie Chaplin, and this was one. I was the tramp making fools of the villains with a simple movement of my wrist and a nod. Laughter breaks down the barriers which separate people. In truth, no one is any better than anyone else, but in the world we know that some people are rich and some are poor, some are smart and some are dumb, some are handsome and some are ugly, some dance with grace, others limp, some carry guns and patrol borders, while others wander with backpacks. When an underdog like me or Chaplin's Tramp evens the score, the whole world laughs.

The roots of humor lie in oppression. Think of the great American comics of the twentieth century. So many have come from oppressed classes and ethnic minorities. Think of Milton Berle, Sid Caesar, Henny Youngman, Woody Allen, Bill Cosby, Richard Pryor, Eddie Murphy, Gilda Radner, Lily Tomlin, Joan Rivers. Jews, blacks, and women all have one thing in common: they are not the recognized majority. They were not born with social power. Some grew up on the Lower East Side of Manhattan or the tenements of Harlem. They were too fat or too skinny, and they learned to survive by making the cold world look at itself and laugh.

My list of oppressions has serious things on it such as my Jewishness, my shortness, my fear of driving, and my lack of direction through high school; but there are also pithy, Andy Rooney-type things such as the phone booths in England, leaky Ford cars and trucks, the plumbing in the house I just bought in Vermont, plastic hangers, zip-lock bags, telephone answering machines, keys and wallets that disappear, bills that don't. Almost any one of these could be the subject of a comic piece.

As Bruce said yesterday, we might not all think of ourselves as humorists, but in our hearts we are all budding Nora Ephrons and Garrison Keillors. We have been hurt, and we have learned how to pull ourselves out and joke about it. It's a natural process. We don't have to force it.

A year ago, my family and I moved to Shoreham, Vermont. We bought a 150-year-old farmhouse in September. It was an old post-and-beam structure encased in aluminum siding with a sagging roof line and L-shaped additions which appeared to be sinking slowly into the mud. A few walls were insulated, and there was a gigantic homemade wood furnace which the previous owner said was his "pride and joy."

By December, we'd been through four cords of wood, and the house was still cold. Not only that, but every time we opened the door to the furnace, the whole house would fill with black smoke. One morning I escaped to my trailer and started freewriting about this furnace. Before I knew it, I had written a comic essay. There is nothing funny about being cold in a Vermont winter or sawing wood to order five times a day or inhaling soot and smoke, but when a pen touches paper we begin to rise above our problems. The universe chuckles.

Woody Allen says, "The worst thing a comedian can do is to try and be funny."

Humor grows naturally out of comic situations and characters who exist in them. Look at the sorrow and annoyances in your life and you will begin to find the comic voice that stands up to bullies and makes the world laugh in joy and recognition.

BL

Follow Through

Here are a few workouts to loosen up the funny bone. Pick one or two and fiddle with them in your journal.

Put a square peg in a round hole. Send a hard-boiled detective to the laundromat with his mother's clothes, or make a beatnik the president of the United States and have him read his inaugural speech. Find a voice or character then slip them into a situation that is totally absurd for them to be in. Then write about it in their voice. For a review of this exercise, go back and read Day Twenty-One.

Steve Martin says that to be funny you have to feel funny. Write when you feel funny or figure out ways to get yourself in a funny mood. Wear funny clothes or talk to yourself in a Daffy Duck voice, or roll around in a tub of lime Jell-O, etc.

Listen and read the masters — new and old. Buy records or borrow them. Read Thurber and Keillor and Ephron and Twain. Imitate their voices on the page. Listen and look for the pauses. Learn that jokes occur often in the spaces between the lines.

Make a list of all the embarrassing things that happened to you that you laugh about now. The more embarrassing then, the more funny now, is the general rule.

Woody Allen says, "When you write humor you don't sit at the grown-ups' table." He's right. So watch children. Sit with them. Especially three- to five-year-olds. Listen to their puns and notice how easy it is to joke with them. Find the child inside yourself and you will find your funny bone.

Infernal Combustion: Life With a Pagan Furnace
(appeared in Country Living Magazine, January 1989)

He sits in the cellar and eats elm stumps like candy. He blows hot smoke at our faces so we smell like kippered snacks and our eyes itch all day. We were normal people in our last house. We heated with oil. We spun a dial and the rooms filled with sweet heat. Now we huddle in the cellar at dawn over old newspapers and chopped cartons as the chimney downdrafts and our huge, homemade wood furnace, Baal, exhales a blast of smoke into our faces.

We bought a tiny farmhouse in northern Vermont in September. Now it's December and we've already gone through four cords of wood. I used to be a writer. Now I sharpen the teeth of chain saws and stalk the dead elm. When people invite my wife and me to dinner, we admire their hardwood furniture, thinking all the time of the splitting maul in the trunk and the pagan god in our cellar waiting for his next sacrifice.

"It's too cold," my wife, Carol-lee says. "I can see my breath." So I run downstairs and load Baal, and an hour later, she is opening windows and shouting, "You are the thermostat! You control the heat by how much wood you put in!"

Downstairs I hear Baal chuckle on a piece of punky pine. I don't argue anymore. When you have a pagan wood furnace in the cellar, you learn that you are always to blame.

I used to have a bumper sticker that said, "SPLIT WOOD NOT ATOMS." Now I spend my mornings hacking away at elm stumps and musing about the possibility of a fission reactor in the cellar. I see my family in clean white suits poised at a control panel in the kitchen, a few stainless steel plutonium canisters where the wood pile now sits. Clean. Efficient.

Sometimes I meet people with normal woodstoves and furnaces. They talk about the joy of splitting wood. They seem calm. They know in their hearts there will be coals in the morning. Orange coals that glow and ask politely for more wood. They are not greeted with a breath of dead ash and Baal's charred echo, "GIVE ME KINDLING, FOOL, AND MAYBE YOU'LL HAVE SOME HEAT BY NOON!"

Nobody understands. They think we exaggerate. They can't understand why anyone would bother to keep a furnace which keeps the heat at 102° in the cellar and 62° in the house. Baal is a jealous god, I tell them. He likes to keep the heat to himself. And besides, we don't have money for an alternative.

This afternoon I get home from work early. I plan to relax with the newspaper under my arm. My wife greets me at the door and hands me yesterday's rolled up newspaper. Her face is smeared with soot, her eyebrows singed. She points silently to the cellar door then trails off into the cloud of smoke that was once the living room. I feel like young Beowulf descending into Grendel's den as I step down the stairway into the cellar. I stoop beneath the pipes and ductwork and run my hands against Baal's lukewarm sheet metal body till I reach his cast iron door. When I open the door, I see a mound of smoldering *Rutland Herald* ash dancing in the smoke and firebrick. Carol-lee's futile efforts to make a fire. Baal speaks:

DRY WOOD. KINDLING. NOW!

But I don't have any.

YOU HAVE FURNITURE. YOU HAVE DRY BEAMS.

The Bank owns most of it.

He snorts a cloud of black smoke into my face and I stumble out the bulkhead onto the lawn.

My wife and I go out for pizza with our three-year-old daughter.

"That furnace is consuming all our time and energy," I say.

"No kidding," she says. "And we'll have emphysema by next spring."

"January."

We weigh the options. A gas furnace from my in-laws. The oil furnace in my old trailer. A prolonged trip to some friendly Caribbean country.

A week later we decide to drive two hundred miles to retrieve the Jotul woodstove my friends Bob and Karen are using to heat their brand-new airtight, passive solar, saltbox house. We arrive at dinner time and the stove is full of coals, so we stand in the living room on the polished hardwood floors and gaze out the thermopane windows trying to contain our jealousy. We make polite conversation for a few hours, then shovel out the glowing coals and carry the stove with pot holders out to the truck.

The next day we put the airtight wonder in the living room and give Baal his sleeping papers.

A month later, the Montreal Express arrives with minus forty degree wind chills. Water pipes in the cellar burst and Baal yawns, ready to come out of hibernation. He doesn't say, "I told you so." He just sits there waiting. He knows we will always prepare the cords of wood for him. He knows he will chew them and spit smoke up the chimney and in our faces. He is from Vermont and we are from the outer regions of ignorance.

Day Twenty-Four:
The Telling Question

Imagine for a moment that a writer is coming to your house this afternoon to interview you. You're shocked because, after all, you're hardly an interesting subject. You're even more amazed when the writer tells you she'd like to profile you. "I'm writing short vignettes of average Americans," she tells you in a brief phone conversation. "Unfortunately, I don't have much time to interview you. Could you write a short autobiography, say, a paragraph or two, that might help me know something about who you are? Don't spend too much time with the background details—you know, where you were born, how old you are, where you live. I can get that information quickly when I see you."

Spend ten minutes composing a brief biography for the visiting interviewer. Think of an anecdote about yourself you think is revealing. Write it in the third person.

If you don't know what to write, go back over the pages of your journal and look for information about yourself that you might find useful. As always, don't agonize over this. Have fun.

Here's mine:

On a typical Sunday morning twenty-five years ago, Bruce Ballenger could be found, unconscious, under a pew at Immaculate Conception Church, a Catholic parish in his hometown of Highland Park, Illinois. He fainted often enough in church that the ushers got used to carrying him out, reviving him in the back room, and sending him back in time for Communion. Now a lapsed Catholic, Ballenger thinks fainting in church has something to do with his interest in writing. "The underside of a pew is a different way of looking at the Catholic experience," he says. "It was horribly embarrassing, but since then I've realized how important it is to me to try to see familiar things in an unfamiliar way. That's what writing is all about.

Seeing What You Said

Was it any more difficult to write about yourself here than elsewhere in the book? Why? Were you surprised at your own biography?

If the interviewer lacked this vignette, what questions might she have asked you that would have prompted you to talk about it?

Writer to Writer

I recently finished a book about lobsters, my favorite food and a symbol of New England's coast, where I now live. When I started, I knew next to nothing about the creatures besides what I learned hanging around lobster pools in fish markets, or in my kitchen, where I would conduct amateur anatomy lessons before and after cooking them. That never stopped me from writing the book, because I knew I was curious enough to find out the things I wanted to know.

Of course, I had to talk to lobstermen, among others, to understand the lives they lead, which, like those of writers, cowboys, and actors, are blurred by popular myth. It was, I confess, a little intimidating. Lobstermen are often reticent and suspicious of outsiders. Though I'm shy, I get along well with most people, including strangers, but I wondered whether I'd have the will to walk down a long wharf and strike up a conversation with someone who would immediately know I was from some distant, land-locked state where lobsters are considered overgrown crawfish.

Before my first interview with a local lobsterman, I thought about what questions I wanted to ask, and made long lists in my notebook. They seemed mechanical, uninspired: How long have you been fishing? What was your best day on the water? What was your worst? How do you feel about new regulations that would increase the minimum size? All through the interview, I rattled off my questions, taking notes on the usually brief responses, all the time wondering why I felt no less a stranger to this man I wanted so much to know.

Toward the end of the interview, I set my notebook aside and asked, almost off-handedly, "Are you going to encourage your son or daughters to get into the lobstering business?"

He paused for a moment, looked down, and stared at his open palms. "No way," he said. "It's too much work for what they'd get out of it."

I knew I was on to something. After an hour telling me what I expected to hear—that the work is hard, but the rewards are plenty—the lobsterman startled me with his remark. "Oh really," I said. "Could you tell more about that?" Then he talked with feeling about the changes in the industry and his fading dreams that someday his children would carry on his legacy.

That chance to say "Could you tell me more about that?" is a magic moment for most interviewers, because it's when their subjects often begin to reveal themselves. It is difficult to know what questions will trigger that moment. Some can't be anticipated beforehand, no matter how thorough a list you make. What I learned that day was how important it is to respond to the people I write about as human beings, not as subjects who can simply be pumped for information. In the same way that we listen to our own voices when we write, we need to listen attentively to the voices of the people we interview for the traces of feeling that hint at who they are. And then we need to respond with our hearts, not just with our notepads.

Look at the short autobiography you wrote in this workout. You might have written, as I did, about something that revealed some significant contour of your life. I used to faint in church when I was young, and found it deeply troubling. I am still trying to sort it out, but know enough to say that, in subtle ways, it has changed the way I see things.

A skillful and attentive interviewer could have found the questions that would have led me back to those difficult Sundays: "When did you decide to become a writer? Did you have an early experience that affected the way you write? Fainting in church? Really? Could you tell me more about that?"

Work backward in the same way from your autobiography. What questions might someone ask that would lead you to start talking about what you wrote?

So far in this book, Barry and I have emphasized personal experience as a rich vein of material for writing. Most writers — fiction or nonfiction — are selfishly fascinated by other people, too. The way I come to see the lobsterman through my writing says as much about me as it does about him.

When you interview people, find ways to expose the face sweating under the mask. It begins with listening, not to what you want to hear, but to what people say and to the timbre of their voices. Then you'll find the questions that will pull you towards that moment when you can say, "Can you tell me more about that?"

BB

Follow Through

Get some listening practice. Call up a friend or a relative, tell him or her that you want to do an interview. Meet at their house, the local cafe, or in the park — someplace relaxed and comfortable. Prepare some questions before-hand, but never feel bound to ask them. Listen carefully (something that may come easier with a good friend than a stranger), and take notes in your journal. Find the questions that will encourage your subject to share anecdotes about their life, perhaps like the short autobiography you wrote for the first part of this workout. Don't finish until you've collected at least three. Remember the questions that allowed you to say, "Tell me more." Save your notes for later.

Day Twenty-Five:
The Telling Line

Go to a public place like a bar or restaurant or airport, any place where people do a lot of socializing and it is easy to eavesdrop without being conspicuous.

Carry your journal and find a place to sit within earshot of some people. Copy down or transcribe as much of their dialogue as you can in fifteen minutes. Be sneaky. Use a tape recorder if you like. Just get the words down.

Look over your transcript. Read it aloud to yourself and circle any bits of dialogue that seem particularly revealing.

Seeing What You Said

Was it easy to do this assignment, or did you feel sneaky?

Could you keep up with the conversation, or was it impossible?

When you look at the dialogue, are there any lines which stick out as particularly telling about the person's personality, or was it all pretty bland? Did the people talk in sentences or fragments? Did their conversation follow one topic or did it skip around? What does the conversation reveal about the relationship between the people?

Writer to Writer

A student of mine once tried to describe a lecherous old fellow named Henry who used to sit hour after hour in the diner where she worked as a waitress. She started with his red suspenders, then his green Dickie workpants, then the Dutch Masters cigars he'd keep unlit in his mouth since he gave up smoking. Though her description was vivid, she kept insisting it was all wrong. The more she tried to describe Henry, the more her description seemed to fall short. I suggested she try remembering as many of Henry's phrases as she could and write them down in her notebook. "Give me a slab of cow pie, and don't put none of that shit whip on it," Henry would say, or "Hey, come over here honey. Do me a favor. Stick your finger in my coffee and sweeten it up a bit."

With just a few lines of dialogue, Henry sprang to life. As a fiction writer, when my characters are going flat, I try to get them talking. I need to hear their voices so I can believe them and they can start believing in themselves.

To write convincing dialogue requires a good ear, and the only way to acquire a good ear is to start listening for the *telling lines* and writing them down. But what is a telling line?

My friend Tom Jenik was in a taxi in New York en route to a job interview. He had an enjoyable conversation with the driver, a Vietnam Vet who, like most New York cab drivers, did not mince his words. Tom wanted to give the driver a good tip, but he soon realized all he had in his pockets was change. He spent a minute digging out his last pennies and handed a fistful of change to the driver. The driver turned to him with a quizzical nod and said, "Ain't it something? The guys that don't got it are the ones that give it."

I was going to write this line down in my notebook but I didn't really need to. A telling line of dialogue sticks to your ribs. As with Bruce's telling question yesterday, it reveals something about the speaker and his relationship with other people, himself, and the world. It sings.

I once wrote a short story about three hobos who lived down the railroad tracks in the town where I grew up. There was a moment in the story where a young boy has a confrontation with one of the hobos and threatens to punch him. It was almost a comic moment in the story—a nine-year-old boy squaring off with this fifty-year-old beer-swilling tramp—but the more I tried to write the dialogue, the more unavoidably serious and melodramatic it became. Part of the problem was that I couldn't remember how fifty-year-old hobos talk and since there aren't any hobos in Dover, New Hampshire, anymore, I didn't have anywhere to go to interview or eavesdrop. I was stuck.

Then one day, weeks later, I was out running with my friend Mike Bonneau. Mike is much faster, and to make matters worse, he's a great storyteller. The conversations we have while running always make me wish I'd brought a notebook and an oxygen bottle. Mike was telling me a story about a high school friend who was a bit of a bully. One day the fellow picked a fight with a grave digger who was about three times his size. He didn't know this, however, until the guy stepped out of his truck and started moving toward him. The grave digger took one look at Mike's friend and said, "Listen Jack, I was streetfightin' while you was still swimmin' around in your daddy's scrotum."

That was it. That was what the hobo in the story needed to say to the boy. It was the perfect threat because it was funny and deadly serious, and it was about fathers and sons. And more than that, it was real. It even seemed original then, though I've since heard it again in other contexts, and I'm not sure it may not even be a cliché in certain circles. Still, this was the telling line for the story, because it reveals the hobo's primitive relationship to his own father and to himself. He was a little fish who grew up in the shadow of a giant, and now that he is a giant, he sees his childhood insignificance in the little boy. A telling line shows more than you can easily explain.

A few months ago I watched a documentary about the Holocaust, called *Shoah*. There was an interview with a man who worked in the Polish resistance around the death camps. He was asked how he was affected by the work he did there. It was a simple question but it triggered a wave of sadness that washed across the man's face. He looked away from the camera, then at the ground, then away from the camera again. I've read many books and seen many documentaries about the Holocaust, but this one man's face and the one simple line he said, as he finally looked directly into the camera, seemed to say more than anything I've ever read or seen.

"If you could lick my heart, it would poison you."

Tune your ears to the voices around you. Sift through the chaos and find the lines that speak to you, which reveal people and their relationships to themselves and the world around them.

BL

Follow Through

Look through the conversation you eavesdropped on. Circle lines which seem revealing. Go back to the interview you did for yesterday's follow-through and do the same thing. Read the lines out loud and listen to your voice. What does it reveal about the speaker's relationship with themselves and the world?

Now ask yourself, "What is bad dialogue?"

It's phony. It's trite. It's characters who seem to say what their authors want them to rather than what's in their heads. Above all else, it's predictable.

Picture Batman and Robin on a conveyor belt heading for a buzz saw. Robin turns to Batman and says, "Holy sawdust, Batman. What are we gonna do?" Batman gets that strained look on his face and says, "If I could just reach my Bat knife . . ." What would these two say and do if they were not simply cartoon characters? If this was real life and they were real people?

Pick two characters and a somewhat clichéd dramatic situation. For example, a husband is leaving his wife or visa versa. Write a flat dialogue between the two, trying to keep in mind the basic principles of bad dialogue writing, i.e., predictability, triteness, phoniness. You may wish to begin, "You never loved me."

What are the worst lines? Why? Which lines seemed to be moving toward good dialogue? Why? How could you change the scene to make it into good dialogue? How could you make it worse?

Day Twenty-Six:
Beyond the Words

Think about someone you really dislike, maybe someone who is arrogant, domineering, manipulative, macho, or rude. (If everyone you know is swell, try imagining an obnoxious character.) Choose one word that best describes the aspect of their personality that bugs you most. Write it in your journal.

Now reconstruct a scene or situation (or make one up) that would show someone who doesn't know this person the aspect of their personality that galls you. *Don't use the word you chose above in your composition.* Let the specifics do the telling. Concentrate on little behaviors, quirks, or habits that reveal the annoying quality. For example, "He strutted into the room with his leather tool belt perched on his hips. The long hammer dangled down one leg like an oversized forty-five. He folded his arms across his chest, and for a moment noticed the abrupt curve of a muscle on his arm. He picked at a pimple. Outside, his pickup truck, large and unblemished, idled in the driveway."

Spend twenty minutes on this.

Seeing What You Said

After reading your composition, could someone guess the word you chose in the first part of the exercise?

Was it hard to resist explaining how you feel about this person?

Does any one detail best show the annoying quality?

Writer to Writer

For my lobster book, I interviewed a well-known scientist, Joseph Uzmann, in his cluttered office at the National Marine Fisheries Service in Wood's Hole. Among other things, he spends a lot of time chasing lobsters in a submersible, scuttling along the bottom in the deep water of the continental shelf. While I waited for Joe to finish a phone call, I noticed he had a Band-Aid over the bridge of his nose. A minute later, a large map over his desk, attached with silver duct tape, came tumbling down. With the phone lodged between his ear and shoulder, he crawled up on his desk and stuck the map back up again. A pile of papers—fat reports and memos—teetered on the edge of the desk and fluttered to the floor. We both lunged.

Before Joe Uzmann had even said a word, he told me about himself—a busy man who barely defies entropy, who remains confidently one step ahead of complete chaos. I was too embarrassed to ask about the Band-Aid that was over his nose, but my guess was that he bumped into something with his submersible.

Yesterday, Barry spoke of the telling line; if we listen carefully enough, the people we write about will reveal themselves to us by the things they say. The same is true if we are attentive to the little things that people *do*—a gesture, a quirk, a habit. I had a friend who walked like he had a tightly coiled spring in his ankles. He took long strides, and at the end of each there would be a noticeable bounce as his heels left the ground, momentarily airborne. I didn't think much of it at first, but later learned he was an avid backpacker. Without a forty pound pack, he seemed to delight in the experience of weightlessness, bouncing down the sidewalk like an astronaut on the moon.

I have since learned to pay attention to the ways people make their way through the world, to the ways that people speak without words. I notice the way Stephanie, a shy student of mine, shakes her foot like the tail of a rattle-snake when she's nervous. I notice the way Brock, a writer friend, often fills in silences by softly singing rock and roll lyrics, as if music is always playing in his head, just below the surface of any conversation and almost every thought. I notice the way Barry seems to always rise from his chair whenever I rise from mine, and sits again when I do. It is, I think, a communal dance, another way that he expresses kinship.

I'm not in the habit of writing about people I *don't* like, so I thought this exercise would be challenging. It was easy. I had no problem thinking of people who get on my nerves, including the electrician who wired our house this spring. He was one of the most arrogant young men I've met. I think the detail in my short composition showing this best is the way he struts across the room like a cowboy, with his leather tool belt clinging to his hips.

The familiar fiction writer's adage — "show don't tell" — applies to nonfiction writers, too. People, whether real or imagined, have much to show us, often unwitting revealed, not only by what they say, but in more subtle things: the disorder of a desk, the unearthly bounce of a long stride, and the choreography of chairs.

BB

Follow Through

It takes practice to look beyond the voices of the people we write about for the more subtle clues about who they are.

Return to your notes from the interview on Day Twenty-Four. Read them over and reflect on the person you interviewed.

Try to come up with one word that captures your strongest impression of him or her. Spend ten minutes freewriting in your journal about where that impression came from. Be as specific as possible. Think about not only what they said during the interview, but how they live, how they handle themselves, how they look.

If you can, spend more time with them, fleshing out more specifics that contribute to that impression (or perhaps suggest another), paying attention to the revealing subtleties we talked about here.

Day Twenty-Seven:
Make a Scene

When people communicate to each other, what they don't say or do reveals as much as what they do. People are complex. They hide things from each other and themselves. Weak writing reveals too much ("you never loved me" or "he anxiously felt nervous"). Strong writing is fueled by secrets and how people reveal or fail to reveal them.

Think of a situation where two characters have a secret from each other. If you can't think of one, use one of these. A husband has just lost his job and his wife is pregnant. Write a dialogue where both characters never reveal their secrets. Just write what the people say. Leave space between each line of dialogue for the Follow Through.

Seeing What You Said

What lines of dialogue seem particularly good? Which lines of dialogue particularly seem bad? Why?

What makes a good line of dialogue? What makes a bad line? How can you change a weak line to make it stronger?

Writer to Writer

I once heard a composer on the radio say that music wasn't notes but the spaces between them. The same might apply for dialogue. It is the spaces between the lines that bring the dialogue to life. For this reason, I end up cutting out a lot of the dialogue I write. I look for the lines that tail off into the white space and let the reader fill in the blanks with their imagination. The best dramatic and humorous dialogue thrives on undercurrents, unspoken pauses that tell us everything we need to know about the characters and their situations. Here's my attempt at the exercise:

"I went to the doctor's today," the wife said.
"Why?"
"Well, I thought we might go out to dinner tonight."
"We haven't been to Burger King in a while."

"I was thinking of some place a little more . . ."
"There's a new Wendy's in town."
"You look tired."
"I had a long day."
"But you're home early."
"I am? Yes . . . I am. So what did the doctor say and did you fill out the insurance forms?"
"Why don't you take a bath, dear?"
"All we have is a shower."
"Right."

Okay, it's not Tolstoy, but looking it over quickly I like the line about Wendy's and Burger King. It tells the reader that all the husband can think about is economics. I don't like the line about the insurance forms. It pushes too hard. I don't respect the reader's intelligence, the reader's awareness of the undercurrents, as I do near the end with the lines about the bath and the shower. That is the strongest dialogue, I think.

I like the way the dialogue hops around, how the husband doesn't answer the wife's question about why he's home early. When people are obsessed with some problem they only half listen to each other and their conversations have a revealing, unfinished quality. I think the dialogue would work better with more of this. It seems a bit too trite, although it is a clichéd situation (though that's no excuse). I like it when each character gets illogical. That's why the final line seems to be heading in the right direction. The wife reveals her nervousness there without me, the author, pointing to it. When you're writing good dialogue, your characters say things you don't expect them to say.

Situations may seem predictable, but the people who act in them are not. The best dialogue proves this. Whether it's a comic scene or a dramatic scene. Good dialogue is always the spaces between the lines, the things left unsaid.

BL

Follow Through

Once your people are speaking, you are on your way to writing a scene. A scene is simply dialogue mixed with action and exposition. At the very least, exposition tells us who is speaking: "I'm home honey," he said as he walked through the door. But when a writer really has control over his or her craft, exposition can help bring the dialogue to life, frame the speaker's words to a time and a place that makes it more real for the reader, and reveal the relationship between what people do and what they say (see Days Twenty-Five and Twenty-Six).

In a climactic scene in Alfred Hitchcock's film *Notorious*, Ingrid Bergman is sitting at a table drinking tea with her kindly aunt who has been gradually poisoning her. The poison is in the tea and the audience knows it. The camera shows the aunt's face as she talks. Then the camera shows Ingrid Bergman's face. Then the camera shows Ingrid Bergman's dizziness. Suddenly, the camera drops to the floor and shows the teacup in profile and Ingrid Bergman beyond it. If we were watching the film in a movie theater, we'd be staring at a twenty-foot teacup. Hitchcock dramatizes the dialogue by framing it with the most important physical detail. He knows what the teacup means to his audience and he lets us see it the moment before Ingrid Bergman realizes her aunt is poisoning her. If he were a writer instead of a film director, the scene might read something like:

> "Have some more tea, dear," said the aunt.
> "Thank you. I don't feel so good," said Ingrid Bergman.
> She felt dizzy. The teacup grew enormous in front of her. It was a bottomless cavern and she was staring into it.
> "You need some more tea, to help with that cold."
> It fell from her hands and shattered on the floor.
> "You're poisoning me," she cried.

Hitchcock uses his camera the way a skilled writer uses exposition. He pinpoints physical details which bring the scene alive. Like Bruce writing about the lobster scientist, Hitchcock finds the actions and details that reveal a situation.

Short story writer Raymond Carver says, "It is possible to write about commonplace things using precise language and send a chill up the reader's spine." A good detail in the right place is worth a hundred scattered over the page.

There are very few writers whose dialogue is strong enough to stand on its own without exposition. Readers like to see who is speaking. They want to pin voices to coffee cups and smokey bars. They want to see, smell, and hear the scene.

Go back over your dialogue and fill it in with exposition. Give your characters a setting to move around in. Show their actions and their inactions. Don't get inside the characters' heads. Think of yourself as a movie director pointing a camera at these people as they speak.

Which bits of exposition do you like best? Which seem to be just filling in the gaps? Which could be cut without leaving a hole? Which help to make the dialogue stronger? Which seem to weaken the dialogue?

Edit your scene and revise it on another page in your journal. Cut dialogue that doesn't work and/or replace it with exposition. Example:

"Bye, Edith. See you tomorrow."

"Bye, Joe."

Replace with: They said goodbye.

Make a scene.

Day Twenty-Eight:
Through the Glass Door

Today you need to go to the local library. Grab your journal and this book and take off. Find a seat somewhere. Freewrite for seven minutes about how it feels to be there, what it makes you think about, or remember.

Write a sentence or two that summarizes what your freewrite seems to be saying to you.

Now test your library skills by finding the answer to one of these questions:

What significant or insignificant thing happened in the nation on the day and year you were born? What are the origins of your first name?

Allow yourself no more than fifteen minutes to find this information. Ask the librarian for help if you'd like.

Seeing What You Said

Do you remember the library as a welcoming place or as an intimidating one? Did your freewrite bring you back to times when you were young, poring through the *Encyclopedia Britannica* for a paper or whispering to a girl- or boyfriend? Did you remember a stern or friendly librarian? Did you write about how much you love books, or the frustration of discovering the book you needed for a term paper was missing from a shelf? In the second half of this exercise, was it rewarding to find out what you needed to know, or were you frustrated because you didn't know where to begin or your library couldn't help you? Did you ask for help? Was it hard to?

Writer to Writer

I always thought that most people who love to write must love books, and if they love books, they must also love the library. Several years ago I told my prose writing students to leave class for twenty minutes and go to the college library to quickly find out what happened on the day they were born. I thought they would enjoy the exercise, and it would help me make a point about how important it is for all writers to know how to find facts fast. Instead, they grumbled and groaned and slid down in their seats. "I hate the library," muttered a student, and heads nodded all around.

Later, I wondered if they always felt that way.

My freewrite reminded me that my first library card had a small metal strip embossed with mysterious numbers that would hold the ink from the machine at the checkout desk. After I checked out a book, I would press the metal against the back of my hand, neatly printing the numbers on my flesh. I don't recall the titles I used to borrow back then, but there must have been many of them because I remember how often my hand seemed stamped with the tiny numerals from my library card.

My hometown public library was fairly large, with a children's and adult section, separated by a large glass door. The children's library had small chairs and tables, and a soft carpet that beckoned, and I would spend hours lying on my stomach turning the pages of colorful books protected by clear plastic jackets. I don't remember any particular librarians, but I do remember they were always women and they were always kind.

The adult library was a fearful place to me then. The bookshelves reached to the ceiling, and the large tables and chairs were a heavy, dark wood, placed in groups on the carpetless floor like muttering old men. The librarians in the adult section, solemn sentries of silence, enforced quiet with a glare or a lone finger to the lips. I was sure that if I mistakenly wandered from the children's section to the adults', their wrath would be directed at me.

It was sixth grade, I think, when I finally passed through the glass door to the adult library without fear. I needed the grown-up encyclopedia for a school report on China. Before long, I was wandering through the stacks as a confident explorer, checking out books on astronomy, bird watching, and even a fat novel now and then.

In college, I haunted the library more from need than desire, and though I wasn't a very efficient researcher (partly because I was too shy to ask the librarian for help), I didn't learn to hate it like many of my students apparently do.

Surprised at their reaction to my research exercise, I asked them why they dreaded spending time in the college library. They told me horror stories about hunting hopelessly for the one book that was essential for a term paper, being confused about where to begin looking for sources, or an upsetting encounter with an impatient librarian.

The place sounded more like a savage wilderness than home territory. I realized later that it easily could seem that way if the library took control of the researcher instead of the other way around. The solution was to give my students more practice with important sources, but first I had to convince them that the library is a gold mine for writers—as memory is—and to avoid it is not only sad, but foolish. It helped to encourage them to remember—like I did, and maybe like you did in the first part of this exercise—that the library was once a welcoming place for many of us, and it can be again.

All writers, including fiction writers, do research. A novelist working on a book set in Victorian England may spend weeks collecting material about the period. My book on lobsters involved substantial research, including following the trail of little-known books on the fishery that were published in the last century. Someone in my writing class recently wrote a personal essay about date rape, and found through her research that her experience was validated by others. It both made her feel better and deepened her own insight.

Other times you only need a quick fact—you're writing an essay on the difficulty of placing a parent in a nursing home and you wonder: How many elderly in this country receive that kind of care? What is the average cost?

All creative activities involve problem-solving, and in that sense, library research is creative, too. It can even be fun, like detective work. You find questions you want the answers to, follow leads, and discover new trails to follow. Like any other aspect of the writer's craft Barry and I talk about in this book, research becomes easier with practice and its joys then multiply.

In the second half of this workout, you confronted a research problem. Asking the librarian for help is not a sign of defeat. When I overcame my shyness, that's how I learned how to use the library, especially the reference section, where the detective work often begins for writers. If you were investigating what happened on the day you were born, you probably found your way to microfilm. There you could pull the strip for the *New York Times*, or some other national newspaper on the date of your birth, and quickly find what you needed to know. Though some small libraries lack microfilm, most have a *Dictionary of Names* in the reference section. The card catalog might have sent you to it (under the heading "Names, personal").

If you wandered around in frustration, cursing this book or Mrs. Honeywell, the stony librarian who kicked you out of the school library for throwing bubble gum in Lindsay Herbst's hair, get it out of your system. Then recommit yourself to research practice. Make the library an ally to your writing, and if it helps, remember the wonder you felt when you finally passed through the glass door and discovered the world in the *Encyclopedia Britannica*.

BB

Follow Through

Try brainstorming a list of subjects that raise questions for you that can be answered through research. Maybe you went to Spain and watched a bullfight. You want to write about the experience, but you wonder how bullfights became such an important part of Spanish culture. Maybe, like Barry, you're writing a short story about what it's like to be dead. You are interested in people who were legally dead but later were brought back to life. What did they say about it?

Try composing a street scene set in your hometown a hundred years ago. Research the period and incorporate as many specifics as you can.

Common Reference Sources for Writers

If research is like detective work, then the reference section of your library is the FBI archives. It's rich with helpful leads and information about what you want to know and where you can find it. Here are sources often used by writers.

For the *most* recent information on any subject use:
The telephone

To find the right people to call use:
The phone book
The Encyclopedia of Associations

For *very recent* information on most subjects use:
The national newspaper index

For *fairly recent (or older)* information use:
The Reader's Guide to Periodical Literature
Other magazine indexes

For *in-depth* information use:
Card catalog
Books in Print
Monthly Catalog of the United States Government Publications
Specialized Indexes (often gives more scholarly sources): Art, General Science,

Biography, Humanities, Education, Social Sciences, Physical Education, etc.

For quick facts use:
Book of the States
Facts on File
Kane's *Famous First Facts*
Guinness Book of World Records
Statistical Abstract of the United States
The World Almanac & Book of Facts

If you're not sure what subject heading to look under, use:
The Library of Congress Guide to Subject Headings

If you're not sure what reference book might be useful, use:
The Guide to Reference Books

Day Twenty-Nine:
The Road Is Chasing Us

You leave the library and a strange feeling comes over you. You thought it was a normal day. You thought you would go home and write, maybe have a little supper, watch a rerun of *Family Ties*. You didn't expect to enter a new dimension; a dimension not of space and time, but of mind. You thought the signpost up ahead would say yield, but instead it said, "The Twilight Zone."

Imagine a planet physically different than the world we live in. Maybe people use turnips instead of money, or women are ten times larger than men, or the streets are paved with Velveeta cheese. Help your imagination by taking notes, brainstorming and clustering. Try naming the world before you start. Make a list of names and pick the best. When you're ready, spend ten minutes composing a short paragraph describing your world.

Seeing What You Said

Did you enjoy making up a new world, or did this seem silly and pointless?

When you look at your new world, has it grown out of your experience or is it totally invented?

What details in your new world make it come alive? Which details seem unnecessary? Can you think of people living in this new world? What are problems they face?

Writer to Writer

I was driving in my 1969 Dodge Dart with my three-year-old, Jessie Lynn. She looked up from her car seat and pointed to the rear view mirror. "Daddy, look, the road is chasing us." I looked in the rear view mirror and saw the road curving and sidewinding its way behind us.

"That's not real," I said. "I mean, it just looks like that, honey."

She nodded, with a slightly confused look on her face and said, "Well, tell that pretend road to stop chasing us!"

Adults see the world through concepts passed down through the ages; children use their eyes, ears, nose, and imagination. Adults know the moon orbits the earth, children know the moon hides behind trees and barns, pokes its head up above mountains, floats up into the sky. Adults *try* to be poets, children are.

When fantasy writer Ursula Le Guin says, "An adult is a child who survived," she is referring indirectly to the many children whose imaginations don't survive crippling educations and burdensome lives. Imaginations wither in adults who see no apparent use for them. Fantasy becomes something people allow in their spare time, or even sadder, when they are asleep.

When I ask students to write fantasy or fiction, their work is often very simple and primitive and, more often than not, they see no need for revision. They don't see fantasy as something they need to make real for the reader as they would with nonfiction material. They think fiction writing is somehow easier because you can make it all up, but they don't understand what children know instinctively: Imaginary worlds can be as real as the ones we live in.

As a fiction writer, I find my work often leans toward the imaginative. I wrote a story recently about men who exist only in the imaginations of women. The story started when I was looking through *Time* magazine and noticed the men in the cigarette ads. They all had cleft chins, smug grins, eyes that were bled of all emotion. I asked myself, "What do these guys do in their spare time? What if these sexy guys only existed in the minds of women? What if these virile men were, in 'reality,' helpless hunks created by the women who imagined them and subject to any thought these women had?"

Thus, the story "Dream Men" was born (see page 118). It is a comic story in which one dream man tries to come to terms with his life as an image in the mind of Sarah, the woman who imagines him. Though it is a weird story about a world that began in my imagination, it wouldn't begin to work if it were not tied to something real. The main character's dissatisfaction with his life as a helpless image connects with all people living in a materialistic society who long for something beyond the appearance of things. Fantasy worlds come alive only when they are linked to reality. *Fantasy is reality, only the rules are changed.*

I'm still trying to write this story about Claire, the dead woman who's been floating around in my imagination for the past few weeks. Part of my problem with the story is trying to anchor her. Let's face it, I don't really know what it's like to be dead and if I were to suddenly find out, I wouldn't finish the story. So I took Bruce's good advice. I've been to the library and found a few books on the subject, and as I talked about earlier, I have experiences and first-hand accounts of people I know to help sharpen my ideas.

The rules of Claire's new world become clearer as I write. I know, for example, that as a dead woman her life is over. She is unable to change anything that happened. I know this is important to the story. Like all of us, she has made a few wrong decisions, and through this story perhaps she becomes conscious of them. The decision has to do with Tom, the man she married. Maybe he wasn't the right choice. Maybe there was someone else. That's all I know about the story so far. The story isn't just about what it's like to be dead. Like all stories, it's about life, or else why would anyone want to read it or write it?

When my students want to write about the planet Zercon I tell them fine, just make sure there are things on this new planet which relate to the planet Earth. Make sure there are smells, sounds, feelings. Give the planet suns and moons and tell me if they're different from the ones I know. Tell me what it's like to be an adolescent male or an insurance salesman on Zercon. Show me the color of the sky, a mother's eyes, or the dirt beneath the Zerconese feet and when you drive down the road on Zercon, and you look in the rear view mirror, does the road stay a safe distance behind you, or does it chase after you like a hungry gray-striped serpent?

BL

Follow Through

Look at your new planet. Circle the details which anchor it to the one we live on. If you don't find any strong ones, try imagining some more.

Here are some exercises to help warm up your imaginative brain muscles.

Do some research at the library or observe some animal. Using what you've learned, write a scene or a simple description from that animal's point of view. (Richard Adams, author of *Watership Down*, spent months researching the life of real rabbits before he wrote about imaginary ones.)

Create a monster or imaginary animal. Brainstorm lists of facts and information about it before you start writing. Read Dr. Seuss for inspiration.

Create a perfect world, a Utopia. Make lists of the details of this world. When you're done, pick a person living in this world and describe "a normal day."

Go to McDonald's or Burger King, or any other public place. Don't eat. Sit there at a booth or table. Close your eyes. Pretend you have just landed from another planet. Write a letter back home.

Find a three- or four-year-old and tell her an imaginative story. Tell it with details that make it real. Watch her eyes grow bigger the more you make it come alive. Listen to your voice grow alive with dreams.

Try creating a new world with one sentence. Then describe that world in closer detail. Write a short prose poem or paragraph. Think of yourself as the hungry artist in this prose poem I wrote as an example.

The Hungry Artist

A hungry artist decided it would be cheaper to paint with words.
"A field of wheat," he shouted at the blank canvas.
And a field of wheat appeared.
"Now some sunlight, but not too much, though. Don't want to overdo it."
And the golden light clung like honey to the field.
"Let's make that wheat into bread," he said the next morning at breakfast time, in a moment of blind inspiration.
"No! Not a field of bread. That's not what I meant."
But it was too late. The dark loaves were already choking the horizon, and the hungry artist was already beginning to cry, "Butter!"

Dream Men

Sarah dreamed me last night, and this morning, as she sits in her office drinking coffee, she remembers the dream. I wear a dark blue sweater that bunches up at the shoulders. I am tall, and I approach her from the shadows of an alleyway. I have a face but she does not look into it. I smile, but it is always an empty smile which will curl into a sneer if she keeps watching. I say something—what do I say? She cannot hear it.

Sarah turns to her desk and forgets me but I am still there, poking along down the alleyway, sticking my head out into the street which waits to be imagined. I don't really like the way Sarah dreams me. I feel a hollowness in the chest, like there are organs missing, a mayonnaise jar where my heart should be, empty milk cartons instead of lungs. The life of an image is tenuous at best. Arms and legs grow into loaves of bread at a moment's notice. Children turn to old men and back to children, then into insects and appliances. You want a little stability in your life. You want to feel like you are getting somewhere, but the road you walk along twists like a snake and chases you. So you run but you don't get anywhere, because your feet have turned to cherry Jell-O. You sleep, but you don't dare dream because you might appear in your own dream, sleeping in the same bed, dreaming the same dream.

I was talking to Phil yesterday. He's being dreamed by this woman named Linda. His legs grow dark and tanned and his biceps swell. Linda has long blonde hair and she's always beckoning him to come nearer, but the nearer he gets, the deeper she sinks into the mattress. Phil is very frustrated with this nightly occurrence, so I tell him, "At least you don't have to spend all night in some smelly alleyway."

Phil looks at me quizzically and I notice his eyes are growing bluer by the second. "Someone is dreaming me again," he murmurs. "Damn it. Don't they EVER wake up, these women?" His shoulders grow broader and hair sprouts like shrubbery on his chest. "It's Carlene," he says. "Always with the hair, that Carlene." He stands and his buttocks swell into a pair of green bikini underwear. Soon he is skipping through the wall and he fades like yellow smoke.

I go for a walk in an unimagined forest. The trees are hairy white shadows. The sky a globe of milk. Lately, I've been trying to figure out who I am apart from the women who dream me. It's puzzling, like trying to see your reflection in a mound of earth. As I walk, the ground turns to asphalt, and sweaty brick walls appear on either side of me. It is dark. Sarah again. She's on her coffee break this time. I can feel her sitting at a gray metal desk. I can just barely smell the bitter tinge of Sanka in my nostrils. My heart beats faster as a tweed sport coat grows from my shoulders. I'm running to the end of the alleyway where she walks, but the closer I get, the longer the alleyway becomes. She turns to me and screams. I could use a good pair of running shoes.

When women are not dreaming us, we don't really know what to do with ourselves. A few of us recently formed a support group. We meet in an old living room someone once imagined then forgot about. It is a small room with a stained sofa and a few wooden chairs.

"Sometimes I feel so helpless," Bruce says. "We need to gain some control of ourselves. I mean, just because we're images doesn't mean we don't have rights." Last week a woman named Sharon dreamed him into a large septic system. He spent a day and a half in the dark under a freshly mowed lawn.

"Maybe there is something we can do," says Mel, but even as he speaks the hair on his head scrolls into a blonde salad and a distant stare sweeps over his face. The next second he floats away shouting, "Madeline, oh my darling. Madeline. Oh my darling."

"The trouble is, we don't even exist in the first place," I say. "We're just illusions."

"I don't feel like an illusion," says Kenneth. He sits on the end of the sofa with his legs crossed. His hair is blown dry. His suit is gray and nicely pressed.

"Well, I know. That's the problem," I say. "We don't even know what illusions are supposed to feel like. Nobody ever tells us. We just are."

"What do men who aren't illusions do?" Jeff asks. He stands by the door stroking an imaginary beard. His Gucci boots are polished to a brilliant shine.

"Beats me," I say. "Maybe they do the same thing we do. Who knows?" In my heart I know this is not true. I see them camped in front a TV slurping beer or jogging solo down a beach. They are happy. No one is imagining them. Their beer guts hang joyfully over their belt buckles.

As I think, the room turns to brick and the sour smells of the alleyway return. Sarah again. Where is she now? A board meeting? The subway? Why can't she leave me alone? I pull the tweed coat tighter over my shoulders. It's gotten colder in the alleyway. I look up at the small rectangle of night sky. Stars shine dully through the haze of pollution. The garbage cans are full of old rags and urine-soaked rugs. Suddenly, a sound behind me. A pair of gloves encircle my neck. I am gasping for air. A woman is screaming at me. "You bastard," she shouts. "I'm gonna kill you. You bastard."

I feel myself dissolving. First my hands, then my legs, then my throat. I begin to float above the alleyway, only it isn't an alleyway at all but a great river. I look down and see myself swimming into the street. A woman in a red dress is swimming after me.

The next second I sit on the sofa. Mel has just returned from the land of Madeline. His hair is mussed up and his face scarred. Long tears run the length of his shirt.

"No comment," he says.

"I just got back myself," I say.

"I can tell," he says.

"Got a cigarette?" I ask.

"No," he says. "You look like you just saw a ghost."

"I did," I say.

"Don't bore me with the details. I got enough problems."

"Why were we born?"

"We weren't born, that's the problem," Mel says. "If we were born, we could at least die."

Silence.

"I think she's in therapy," I say.

"Who?"

"Sarah. You know—alleyway Sarah."

"That's trouble."

"I know."

Mel was once imagined by a woman named Claire. She went into therapy and the next week he found himself hanging naked from piano wire in the lingerie section at K-Mart.

"What do I do?" I say.

Mel looks at me. He rubs the long scars on his cheeks and smiles at the blatant absurdity of my question. I pour myself a glass of water. The room melts like butter around us.

It's the alleyway again, and my body inside the trench coat. At least I think it's my body, but it's too dark to tell. I begin to whistle an unfamiliar tune in a minor key. I look up at the sky, but it has not been imagined and there are gaping sores where the stars should be. "Sarah," I whisper. "I'd like to chat with you, if you don't mind." My voice is higher than it should be and I notice my fingernails have grown. I wear fruity perfume. I have a large kitchen knife in my sequined purse. I see a man walking my way from the street. The man smiles, a smug sort of smile, as he stuffs his hands into his pockets. I take out my knife. I am going to stab the man in the heart. The man is me.

The alleyway fades.

My dress makes a big hit with the guys in the support group.

"Dig those legs," says Mel. "Hubba hubba."

"Please, it's been a difficult morning," I say.

"I don't get it. She turned you into a woman. Ain't that odd?" says Bruce.

"No, it ain't odd at all. She's in therapy. Remember."

There is a short doleful silence, as though they are all mourning the loss of a dead friend, then titters of laughter as I try to disconnect my gold hoop earrings from my swollen lobes.

"You want a pair of wire cutters?" Mel asks.

"Very funny."

In bed that night I think hard about Sarah. Maybe if I try hard enough I can even dream her. Then she'll really know what it feels like. I see her legs, long and sensuous, her cheeks like ripe apples, her lips curling into a smile. "Talk to me, Sarah," I whisper. "Can't you see? I'm just an ordinary guy who wants to come out of his alleyway to meet you." I wait under the covers for an answer. I whisper some more things along the same lines.

Nothing.

I wake up in a strange bedroom on a double bed. There are pink flowers on the wall and a digital clock radio chatters beside me. There is a woman lying next to me and instinctively I know who it is. She rolls over, her eyes still closed, her lips in the kissing position. I try to move, to reach for the lock of hair which dangles over her forehead and slide it back behind her ear, but my hands are bound behind my back and my neck is chained to the pillow.

"I hate you," she whispers.

"Why?" I ask.

"You're just like all of them," she says.

"How?"

"I don't need to talk with you. I really don't."

"You created me. You could at least have the common decency to say a few words to me."

She rolls over and my head falls back onto the pillow. My legs turn to vanilla pudding.

"Sarah," I shout. "Please."

"Go away. You bore me."

"I can't go away. There is nowhere to go, and besides, I'm chained to the bed, and besides that, my legs are pudding, and besides that, I love you."

The words escape my lips before I can think of what I'm saying.

"You what?"

"I love you."

The room melts away and I'm back with the support group, naked on the couch, bound hand and foot.

"It was a productive night," I say.

"Don't tell me. She proposed to you," Mel says.

"No. But I told her I love her."

They cannot hold in their laughter. Kenneth is the worst. He rolls on the floor in his leisure suit. Mel spits up popcorn on the rug.

"I wish you two lovebirds all the happiness in the world," he says, dangling the chains which hang over my ankles.

"You guys can laugh, but for a minute there I didn't feel like an image. I felt— I felt . . . real."

The word is like wind against candle flames. Even the room seems to flicker a moment, the sofa fizzling into the tan carpet, then foaming up again. A bewildered look sweeps over their faces.

"Well, you're a real nice guy," Phil says. "Do you want us to find a real hacksaw and get you out of here? Your legs are real vanilla pudding, too. Maybe we should get some real whipped cream and have a real party."

I get the urge to go for a walk, then I look at my legs and the urge stops. A moment later I am gone, standing with new legs on a beach. It's a gray day and a woman is walking toward me. The woman is dressed in a gray flannel business suit, but instead of a briefcase she carries a submachine gun.

"Hi Sarah," I say.

The bullets whiz through me and I keep walking.

"You die, sucker," she yells.

"Something bothering you?"

My feet turn to tree stumps and my fingers gnarl into branches.

"Sarah, I know you love me. Why must we go through this silly charade?"

Her machine gun turns into a chain saw and she yanks at the starter coil. She cuts me up into four-foot lengths and lets the tide wash over me.

"You're cord wood, baby," she whispers. "I'm through with you."

"You know how I feel about you," I say through the foam. She strides away into the sunlight.

I swagger in the tide for a minute or two, until the ocean fades and I find myself standing on a subway at rush hour. I look down at my hands. I count the fingers. Ten. I know she is somewhere in the vicinity, but I decide not to look beyond the tangle of elbows and shopping bags. I will play it cool.

The next moment I am in an air-conditioned office. A woman's voice, not hers, says, "Describe him to me."

"He's tall and lean," Sarah says. "He's like a man you see in a magazine ad for some stupid cigarette. He's got that smug, I've-seen-it-all-and-I'm-still-miserable look. He hides in alleyways and he waits to jump out at me, but the expression never changes, the blue eyes stay frozen. He makes me so angry I want to scream. I want to tear the hair from his chest just to see if the pain makes any impression on him. I want to step on those ice eyes with my spike heels and watch them shatter."

"Where is he now?"

"I left him at the beach. I cut him up with an imaginary chain saw. But even on the way over here on the subway I could sense him near me. It's a feeling I get, a creepy feeling. I want to scream. I want to hurt somebody."

"Wait a minute!" I shout from the corner of the room. "That's not me she's talking about. I love her. I'd do anything for her."

The woman doesn't hear me. How can she? I'm not real. I'm just something Sarah dreamt up. But this pain in my chest, did Sarah dream that up too?

"I want you to think of this man," the woman says. "I want you to imagine every detail of him. I want you to send him on a rocket ship to outer space. I want you to twist open the hatch for him now and tell him to get out."

"Get out," Sarah whispers.

"Louder."

"Get out," Sarah shouts.

"Louder!"

"GET OUT!"

I think about Sarah often. I squint through clouds at oceans and continents in an effort to catch her micro-shadow walking down a sidewalk or along a beach. The other day Mel floated by, dressed in shorts with red whales printed on them. He was clinging to some chiffon drapery and humming an unrecognizable tune. I called to him against the black sky and he turned to me, his head framed with stars. He tried to speak, but his lips were sewn together with what looked like mint-flavored dental floss. I waved to him and he nodded, his face twisted with recognition.

Every once in a while, I get the feeling someone down there is dreaming me. Blood starts to simmer inside me. Hair grows like grass on my pale legs, and a fisherman knit sweater begins to spin itself round my arms. Then the feeling goes away, my mind gets pale as Crisco and I count the stars, one by one, thinking about the hour I will become a real man and dream about Sarah.

Day Thirty:
Seeing the Man in the Moon Again

Draw a line down the middle of a journal page.

On the left side, brainstorm a list of big, seemingly inexplicable ideas. Things like life, love, God, war, sex, beauty, religion, death.

On the right side, brainstorm a list of specifics. Try listing anything that comes to mind concerning food, sports, astronomy, writing, whatever. Don't worry about being silly (actually, the sillier the better).

Now fill in this sentence, using a word from the left column and specifics from the right:

_____ is a _____ .

Then add a sentence to explain the comparison.

For example, "Religion is a crater. It was formed by the impact of a heavenly body, and people have been falling into it ever since."

Seeing What You Said

Were you surprised by the unlikely comparisons?

Did any seem remarkably apt?

Writer to Writer

A few years ago, I was watching a public television program about a local poet. He spoke to a class of second graders, and before reading one of his poems he asked the students, "Now, what *is* poetry? Does anybody know?" Hands sprouted everywhere. The poet pointed to a boy in the back, who leapt to his feet and said confidently, "Poetry is words that sing."

A few days later, I asked my college English class the same question. There were no sprouting hands, not even a murmur. I called on Alice, who had at last tentatively raised her hand. "Well, I'm not sure exactly what you mean by the question, but I think that maybe poetry could be described as a limited form of prose where the line is the basic unit instead of the paragraph and meaning is often implicit."

Not a bad answer, but I thought the second grader was more on the money.

When Barry's three-year-old daughter, looking into the rearview mirror, observed that the road seemed to be chasing them, I was reminded of the poet and his audience of seven-year-olds. Since the beginning of this book, we've talked about the need for writers to find ways to break their habits of seeing. Children do it with a spontaneity that often startles me.

If Aristotle is right that true intelligence is marked by the ability to make metaphors, then children are blessed with that brilliance. They see metaphors everywhere, which is why the moon looks like cheese, and a shoe is a boat, and eyebrows are like bridges across two pools. Then they grow up, and some of them become English majors, and the moon is the moon and poetry is a limited form of prose with the line as the basic unit instead of the paragraph.

Does this have to be? Of course not. One of the purposes of freewriting, brainstorming, and clustering is to free the child within all of us and reclaim our imaginations. By now, hopefully, you've had the joy of seeing your words rush to the page—with all their childish awkwardness—and been surprised at what they helped you to see. Maybe it happened in this exercise, too, and you found yourself making a surprising connection between a vague idea like love and something as concrete as salami.

Too much thinking can be the enemy of imagination. I know that's especially true for me when it comes to metaphors, or similes, which are briefer comparisons of unlike things. The more I *try* to be metaphorical when I write, the more impossible it becomes. Metaphors, like horses to water, can't be forced (or, like this sentence, they turn up as clichés). More often, I stumble upon a surprising connection in a rush of words; and when it does happen, when I find a metaphor or simile that seems just right, I feel a special kind of joy that must be what makes people want to be poets.

A week ago I mentioned my struggle with an essay about my father's alcoholism. It began as fifteen manuscript pages. It was too long, unfocused, and, it seemed to me, drained of feeling. One June morning, while my wife was still sleeping, I shuffled over to my desk to try one last time to resuscitate the draft. I began in my journal, talking to myself about the piece, and suddenly I found myself remembering my twenty-first birthday, and a rose bush my father gave me as a gift. I planted that rose bush in the side yard, but my father never lived to see it bloom the next spring.

Though I am often moved by what my writing tells me, I am rarely moved to tears; but that morning I cried as I realized that I was like the rose bush, and that he would never see me grow into a young man who loved writing as much as he did. The metaphor ends the essay, and gives it a poignancy that still tightens my throat when I read it (see page 149).

A good metaphor is like that — it surprises, and it gives a refreshing clarity to things that seemed inexplicable. It laughs in the face of logic (after all, people are not roses), and reminds us all what it's like to be a second grader defining poetry, or three years old and captivated by the asphalt serpent in the rearview mirror.

BB

Follow Through

The more we greet the world with the openness of a child, and invite the kind of madness that comes when words rush pell mell to the page, the more likely we are to find metaphors. Try these to induce metaphor madness:

Repeat the earlier exercise, but this time work with a feeling instead of an idea. Think about how you feel at this moment (tired, frustrated, giddy, etc.). Put it in the nucleus of a cluster and see what grows from it. Concentrate on images and things. Complete this sentence with your most interesting comparison: I feel as _____ as a _____ .

Here's an exercise suggested by Gabrielle Lusser Rico, in *Writing the Natural Way*. She suggests that one of the most revealing comparisons we can make about ourselves is with animals. If you were an animal, what would you be? Cluster the word "animal" for a few minutes. Choose one, and cluster again, allowing as many associations to branch from it as you can. Then begin writing in the first person, and be the animal ("I am a panther . . ."), drawing on the material from your cluster.

Learn to see the man in the moon again. Go outside tonight and see if you can. Take a walk this afternoon, find a place to sit, and freewrite in your journal, paying attention to how things look like something else: how an elm is like a wine glass, how the ice on the pond is like lily pads, or how the chrome grills on some cars seem to smirk.

Go to a modern art museum and look at abstract paintings or sculpture. Freewrite in your journal about what they help you to recognize in the world you know.

Go back through your journal and reread some of the freewrites you've done in the past thirty days and hunt down metaphors and similes that, like flecks of gold, may be buried in your plainer prose.

Day Thirty-One:
Tackle a Sheep

Now that you know something about metaphors, it's time to learn about dreams, those coded metaphors that entertain and terrify our sleeping hours. This exercise may take a few days and you'll have to sleep on it. Keep your notebook by your bedside for a week and scribble down your dreams as soon as you get up. Don't be afraid if your dreams don't make sense or if you can only remember tiny fragments. The act of writing will, in most cases, help you to remember more and more.

Find one dream which is particularly provocative and write it again at the top of a fresh page in your journal. Read it over several times, letting your imagination return to the place of the dream.

Now, revise the dream in some way to make it stronger. You might want to begin by finding the moment in the dream which seems to be the core, or simply describe the general feeling of the dream. You might wish to create the dream in more detail, or change the events in the dream to suit how you really want to feel or how you interpret it now. Let your imagination play with the dream like a child with a crazy toy. Do Bruce's core-finding exercise (Day Nineteen), try freewriting or clustering first, or just dive right in. Make the new dream come alive on the page.

Seeing What You Said

Was it hard to make the dream real, or did you dive right in?

How did your dream change when you revised it? How did it stay the same? Did it make more sense after you revised it?

What is the overall feeling of the dream? Did it change in revision?

Can you think of other dreams to revise? Could you invent another dream about the same feelings?

Dreamer to Dreamer

Last night I was playing football. I was a split end and I went out on a fly pattern. I caught the ball and started running, then the field disappeared and I was running along a grassy plateau above the Serengeti Plain in Africa. I could still see the goal line, however, and when I glanced over my shoulder I saw that a big sheep was in hot pursuit. I dove for the end zone and the sheep tackled me. I had made it. The next second I was at a piano, writing music. A song was composing itself. I liked the song. Then I was sitting in the office of an art history teacher I had known years ago. "All I want to know is, what do you think of your music?" he asked.

I replied, "I think I could make a living writing it."

"What do you mean, you think you COULD?" he asked. "You can!"

Then my first musical was being performed on Broadway. It's called *Street People* and I am being billed as the new Sondheim. I watch from the audience as two bag ladies sing,

You have to be so discreet,

to live upon the street,
You must be so debonair
to do all your ironing on a stair.

At this point, the alarm clock went off. I was disappointed. Here I was, at the pinnacle of my career, and I had to wake up and go feed the chickens. Nonetheless, I had achieved a few things. I had outrun a sheep to the end zone and become a success on Broadway all in one night. I was proud of myself.

I told the dream to my wife, Carol-lee, and she informed me it was all my anxiety about functioning as a competent adult. I tried to explain to her that I felt it was more about creativity, the childlike creative impulse in me.

She said, "Darling, you were tackled by a sheep. Doesn't that mean anything to you?"

"But I made the touchdown."

"Yes, dear, you made the touchdown."

Carol-lee majored in psychology. It wouldn't bug me as much if she wasn't always a little right, but she usually is.

In my mind I did Bruce's cut and paste exercise with this dream. I cut the dream into moments and searched for the core. It was easy to find. It was the moment when my former art history professor turned to me and said, "What do you mean, you think you COULD? You can!"

I could feel waves of doubt melting from me, and suddenly I was an instant success. Interestingly enough, the professor who appeared in the dream was a man who wasn't very successful and struggled with massive doses of self-doubt. I remember him telling me it once took him three weeks to write one sentence in his dissertation. I remember observing many times how unhappy he seemed. He was not a man I looked up to in real life, nor was he an inspiring teacher, but here he was, turning up in this dream to tell me how great I was. Wasn't that odd?

Dream images are like metaphors that way. Some are pretty straightforward, others just pop up out of nowhere and make us see things in a new light.

In fiction writing, characters' dreams help make their conflicts come alive. A man can think, "I am afraid of flying in a plane," but if he dreams about falling through thick layers of cumulus clouds, the man's fear becomes tangible for the reader.

Recurrent dreams tell us how characters change. If a prizefighter dreams, night after night, of becoming a priest, the reader knows this is a man with a struggle. If a woman turns around in a nightmare and assaults her attacker, we know she has found a new power which will perhaps affect her relationship with a "real" man in the story. In my story "Dream Men," Sarah's therapy, a conscious practice, puts her in control of her dreams and her life. The more we think about dreams and write about them, the more we own them.

As Bruce indicated yesterday, we have big brains but we are trained to use only a small portion. As in freewriting, clustering, or brainstorming, things have a way of surfacing in dreams. But if we are not in the habit of standing back and looking at our dreams, we can't begin to decode them and understand their wacky logic. Here's my revision.

A sheep is running for a touchdown and I am chasing it. We are on a grassy plateau above the Serengeti Plain in Africa. I tackle the sheep, but as he falls to the ground, I notice a zipper on his belly. I zip it open and out pops my former art history professor. He asks me what I think of my songs. I say I think I could make a living writing them. He says, "What do you mean you think you COULD? You can!"

He climbs back into his sheepskin and trots away.

I am at the Broadway premiere of my latest musical called *Street People*. Carol-lee is with me in the front row. The stage fills with street people, who sing the lead song. "You have to be discreet, to live on the street./You must be debonair/to do all your ironing on a stair . . ."

At intermission, Carol-lee tells me the play has adolescent tendencies. Street people fascinate me because they are homeless. They don't have mortgage payments. I tell her it is about tackling sheep, conquering my need to be like everyone else.

Next, I am running on a grassy plateau again in the sunshine. All is happy until, suddenly, I get the feeling I am being chased. I look back and there is a herd of sheep, and they look vaguely like everyone I've ever known or loved. I stop running and turn to their bleating faces. I wait for them to trample me, but they stop dead and just stare at me.

I look into their eyes. I am not afraid.

In revision, I realized that running for the touchdown was running away from something. Carol-lee was a little right. I have anxiety about being a writer. I think it is an adolescent activity, yet I know it is what I was put on this earth to do. I need to get beyond doubts and ghosts of old teachers. When I can believe in my work it will flow out of me.

At the end of the new dream, I am about to realize there is nothing to fear, nothing to run away from. I can believe in my writing without fleeing this faceless society which would rather I pump gas or sell computers or perform brain surgery.

There is a sheep farm across the street from my house in Shoreham, Vermont. Often when I go to the mailbox to send off a story or field a fresh rejection, I pause and look at the woolly creatures. They look up when they notice me staring. They look confused and just a little curious. They want me to mind my own business. They want to know why I don't eat grass. I hadn't thought of them as the sheep in my dream until just now, as I write this.

That's what dreams are about. They take us by surprise, and like our best writing, they begin to show us who we are.

BL

Follow Through

Think of a character tormented by some sort of problem. One who is afraid of spiders, or one who can't sleep. He was fired from his job. He is a hemophiliac who's just landed a job in a razor factory. Now put them to bed and give them a dream. Don't worry if it's the perfect dream, just give them a dream. Use your own dreams or your own problems as resources. When you've written a page or two, stop. Circle the key moments in the dream and the best details.

Now think of the same character, in the process of overcoming their problem. Revise the dream, accenting parts and adding new information to show their progress.

Day Thirty-Two:
Weed a Sentence and
Make It Bloom

You think metaphors and dreams have no place in the things you write. You write memos. You write reports. You are with the Institute for the Facilitation of Myriad Methods for Sentence Improvement. You give speeches (long ones) to august bodies about the need to initiate a national program for the distribution of a free thesaurus to every fifth grader in an effort to elevate their comprehension of the multiple alternatives in English diction, so essential in light of the egregious decline in contemporary language standards.

The following sentences are in fairly clear, economical prose. You hate clear, economical prose.

Spend five minutes rewriting the sentences to make them stylistically acceptable to the Institute, adding as many words as you can without adding information. See if in the rewrite you can double the number of words in the original version.

> When writing, always keep a dictionary nearby. (Seven words)
> It is hard to find the right word among many possibilities. (Eleven words)
> Irving called a meeting to discuss the right way to spell "separate." (Twelve words)
> Teachers should instruct children in grammar at an early age. (Ten words)
> The dog stole my slipper, then dropped it into the toilet. (Eleven words)

Do your rewrites sound awful? Good. Go back over them, bracketing places in your sentences where you use several words when one will do. Then circle every form of the verb *to be* you used (is, was, were, am, be, being, been).

Seeing What You Said

Did you find it easy or difficult to turn decent writing into pig slop? Did your rewrites sound anything like you? How would you describe the voice — distant, detached, inhuman? Where have you encountered similar use of language? Why might someone deliberately write this way?

Writer to Writer

I received a memo recently from a faculty committee at the university where I teach. It included this sentence: "While those of us in administration are supporting general excellence and consideration of the long-range future of the University, and while the Senate and Caucus are dealing with more immediate problems, the Executive Committee feels that an ongoing dialogue concerning the particular concerns of faculty is needed to maintain the quality of personal and intellectual life necessary for continued educational improvement." (Try reading *that* out loud quickly without taking a breath.)

I'm not exactly sure what that sentence means, but I think the writer is saying that the faculty should talk more about stuff.

The past few days we've been renewing our imaginations through metaphor and dreams, trying to recover a childlike way of looking at the world that makes it come alive for us. That's really what this book is about—the need, through writing, to break our habits of seeing, and bring something fresh and surprising to the page. What you conceived in this workout was more likely the opposite: more dead than alive.

From Day One, Barry and I have encouraged you not to judge too soon, to be playful, open-minded, and to accept that the words you find might be awkward. You will write badly. Even your messy journal writing is probably better than the lumbering passage from the faculty memo, which is self-conscious, pretentious, and downright dense. Take comfort in the realization that some people write badly on purpose and think they're writing brilliantly. These are often the same people who complain bitterly about the decline of English usage and demand back-to-basics writing programs in schools that emphasize grammar and mechanics. They think the bigger word is always better, and mourn their limited vocabularies. They believe that good writing is words dressed up for the ball, rather than those that dance in simpler garb.

All the junior and senior high school teachers I can remember believed this—another reason I hated writing. I spent all my time worrying about *how* I said it, instead of thinking about what is really important: *what* am I trying to say?

That's why Barry and I have said little so far about sentences. Some of you are just waiting for the chance to worry about them, which may freeze your pen and numb your imagination. This is not a pitch for bad grammar. Most of us write to communicate, and the words you choose and how you arrange them make a big difference to readers. It's not whether but *when* you worry about such editing that's important: do it after you've figured out what you're trying to say. Until then, give yourself permission to write sentences that would have drawn red "awks," like vultures, in the margins of your school papers.

When you are ready to edit, don't be haunted by Barry's Grammar Police. You can strengthen your sentences without feeling you deserve a jail term. You can even learn to do it by deliberately writing garbage. I hope this workout will prove that.

Here are my rewrites, all of which are truly awful.

Original: When writing, always keep a dictionary nearby. (Seven words)
Rewrite: When composing written language, a dictionary is an invaluable device and should always be readily available for consultation. (Eighteen words)

Original: It is hard to find the right word among many possibilities. (Eleven words)

Rewrite: It is extremely taxing to locate the correct word when there are a multitude of possibilities from which to choose. (Twenty words)

Original: Irving called a meeting to discuss the right way to spell "separate." (Twelve words)

Rewrite: A meeting was convened by Irving to initiate a discussion that would focus on the proper spelling of the word "separate." (Twenty-one words)

Original: Teachers should instruct children in grammar at an early age. (Ten words)

Rewrite: Young people need to be introduced to the vagaries of sentence construction, diction, and spelling as an early educational experience. (Twenty words)

Original: The dog stole my slipper, then dropped it into the toilet. (Eleven words)

Rewrite: My canine surreptitiously made off with my household foot covering and then took it to the toilet basin, where it was unceremoniously deposited. (Twenty-three words)

I had fun doing this. Though it might have seemed a bit silly to you, deliberately writing badly reveals much about writing well. Two things that burden most poorly composed sentences are passive voice (usually detected by finding the "to be" verb and its variations) and what William Zinsser calls "clutter" (saying in two words or more what can be said in one, or using a long word when a short one will do). When you reviewed your dreadful sentences you probably found a healthy helping of both. They are easy to fix. Think of your sentences as a garden. Clutter, like weeds, obscure the flowers — the important information — and they need to be pulled. Jettison the "to be's" by putting the subject of your sentence up front and making it more alive, more vibrant. (For example: *The cat was kicked* vs *Rockefeller kicked the cat.*)

It may sound as if I'm a good gardener. I'm not. Several weeks ago I received a copy-edited manuscript from my publisher. When I sent it in, I carefully edited it. I was shocked to see nearly every page covered with blue marks — mostly clutter, unnecessary words that grew so thick I confused them with the important things I was saying. At first, I felt like I was back in high school English. I was depressed. But then I began to see the patterns (for example, I love to say "tends to," a useless phrase; I often unnecessarily begin sentences with "but"; and I frequently flirt with the passive voice). Now I am starting to recognize the weeds from the flowers in my sentences. It takes practice.

What about writers, like the author of my faculty memo, who deliberately use clutter, passive voice, euphemism, big words, and dull phrases? For academics, lawyers, and bureaucrats, it can be a kind of tribal language to write that way. Some write in a code that only others familiar with it can crack. Politicians and generals protect themselves with the ambiguity of imprecise language. When a politician says, "We must push this to a lower decibel of public fixation," he really means that he wishes people would get off his back. More often, bad writing simply reflects sloppy thinking. I can always tell when my students are confused or have run out of things to say when their writing falls apart.

When serious writers scrutinize their sentences, they have this in mind: make every word count. If it doesn't, pull it out. Do this often enough, and you may find a sadistic joy in attacking clutter and, in the process, discover a truer, more natural voice in your writing that blooms stronger than ever before.

BB

Follow Through

Return to the draft you finished on Day Nineteen, or any of your other drafts that need editing.

Choose a page and edit it for passive voice, clutter, and murky language. Cut *at least* seven words.

For fun, share your awful rewrites of the sentences in this exercise with a friend. Have him or her try to edit it back down to clarity. See how close he or she comes to the original version.

Spend a minute finding a shorter word or phrase for the following:
- At the present time
- Implement
- Due to the fact that
- He totally lacked the ability to
- Initiate
- In many instances
- Facilitate
- In spite of the fact that
- Individuals
- In a curious manner

Day Thirty-Three: No Facial Expressions for a Month, Please

The flowers are blooming in your sentences. Unlike certain politicians, you are beginning to understand the difference between dissemination of misinformation and a lie. But you are too close to your writing to really know what it says, and how it sounds.

Try this one. Find a piece of writing you've been working on for a while. Type it up or print it neatly. Complete it the best you can. Now, make a list of your closest friends or acquaintances. Pick the one you'd most like to read your piece. Give him a call, mail it, or just drive over and deliver it in person. If you really feel brave, read it out loud.

Notice the feeling of your fingers letting go of the manuscript. Listen to your heart pound. Don't wait around. Let her read in peace.

Sit down somewhere with your journal and freewrite for ten minutes about what it felt like to give up your manuscript to another pair of eyes.

Get back to your reader as soon as possible. Ask him one simple question. "What did you think of my piece?" Then listen. Don't interrupt. Don't grovel or ask for sympathy or get defensive. Just listen.

When he's talked himself out, ask one simple question: "What do you want more of and what do you want less of?"

Later, when you are at home or alone, freewrite ten minutes about your piece and any plans you have for revision.

Seeing What You Said

Was it fun to have somebody read your work, or was it agony?

Did you get indignant at their criticism or did you find part of yourself nodding in agreement?

Did your reader praise anything in your work or was she totally negative?

When you left your reader, were you excited about revising your piece or were you discouraged? Was your final freewrite helpful?

Writer to Writer

Today, I read a few pages of my completed short story "The Last Day" to my friend Roland Goodbody. We sit on a friend's lawn in Portsmouth, New Hampshire, and the wind blows the trees full of spirit. Roland has a nasty cut on his forehead from a near-fatal car crash last weekend. As I read, I am aware of the irony of reading a story about a woman who died in a car crash to a man who just rolled his Dodge Dart on Interstate 89.

In my voice I hear the familiar need for approval. I find myself screening sentences before I read them, leaving out adjectives, cutting lines of dialogue that suddenly look too sappy. Roland frowns as I read. I wonder if the sun is in his eyes or one of his splitting headaches has returned. In my heart I know the real reason. He hates my story. Every last word of it, every last syllable. It is possibly the worst piece of writing he has heard in years. How will he humor his good friend? What will he say?

There is a short silence when I finish the excerpt.

"So what do you think?" I say. My heart jumps into my throat.

"I don't know," he says. "It's weird. It reminds me of some 'Twilight Zone' thing. Something bothers me about it. I'm not sure."

"Can you be a little more specific? Was it the beginning?"

"Yea. The whole thing. I mean, I didn't think it worked like it should. It was too at a distance."

"Should I have put it into first person?"

"I don't know. The 'she this, she that' bothered me. I wanted her to be a real woman. You know what I mean. I guess that's what made it seem like a 'Twilight Zone' thing."

Something is shriveling inside me like plastic in a candle flame. In the silence I look at Roland. He seems cold and distant. No friend of mine. Maybe this accident has reshaped his personality. I force myself to ask one more question.

"Was there anything you liked in the story?"

"Yea. I like the whole idea a lot. How she floats around, and all that stuff in the supermarket is marvelous. I liked that, and it's beautifully written."

My heart finally stops trying out for the tympani section of the New York Philharmonic and my eyes barely water. Roland's brief reaction to a few pages of my short story is starting to make sense.

Seeing the power of a piece illumines the weakness. If I were not an experienced writer, I would not have pushed Roland to tell me what he liked. I would have accepted his negative remarks as proof of my ineptness instead of what it was—valuable wisdom which will eventually help me to revise the story.

Good criticism is a seed which the critic plants in the writer's mind. Praise is the water which allows that seed to germinate. The best critique is almost useless if it does not activate the writer's internal critic. This can be done by acknowledging the writer has not been wasting his time, that there is something good on the page, which cannot be denied. I'm not saying good readers delude writers; rather, a good reader empathizes with the writer's vision, sees beyond the words to what the writer is trying to achieve with those words. Good readers ask questions and make writers see where they have succeeded and where they have failed. And most of all, good readers make you want to write.

My mother was my first valued reader. I would bring home a thing I'd written at school and she'd type it up on her old black Royal and hang it on the refrigerator. They were usually corny assignments with titles like "Happiness Is" or "Sadness Is," but they were the first things I had written, and my mother's uncritical praise motivated me much more than the astute judgments of my writing professors many years later.

Writing teacher Peter Elbow says that to be good critics, writers must learn to play both the believing game and the doubting game when they look at their work. The believing game has to do with basic faith that you have something to say. The doubting game is about questioning the effectiveness of your writing. When I hand a story to a reader, I immediately start playing the doubting game. Sometimes I even lapse into global despair (i.e., Roland won't like my story. Who cares? The world will end in nuclear holocaust soon anyway). A more constructive kind of doubting was the kind I did when I edited sentences in my head as I read. This doubt led to action, helped me to see the power and weakness of my words.

A big mistake young writers make is seeking out readers and critics before they are ready to stop playing the believing game. The best criticism from a skillful reader will only offend or discourage if you are not ready to distance yourself from a piece of writing and play the doubting game. Even seasoned writers struggle to gain distance. I remember my friend, fiction writer Rebecca Rule, handing her novel over to a trusted friend and saying, "No facial expressions for a month, please."

When we show someone our writing, we put ourselves in a very vulnerable position. It's like stripping naked in front of a crowd and asking, "Is there anything wrong with me?" If the audience is not sensitive to their powerful position, even their best wisdom will only offend or confuse. The best critics share their frank judgments with sensitivity.

Tonight I show my completed story to my wife and best editor, Carol-lee. She tells me it's about time and asks why it took me so long. I give her my usual response. I wasn't ready to hear criticism, especially the honest, good kind she would give me.

"You never share things with me," she says.

I hand her the story and climb into a hot bathtub.

As I soak, I can hear her flipping through the pages in the next room. I think about the story page by page. I imagine Carol-lee's big green eyes reading each word. I think about Roland's criticism and my frustration with making Claire real. By the time I towel myself dry, I know the story is not completed at all.

"It's very well written," is the first thing Carol-lee says. "And the concept is pretty complete."

"I know," I reply. "A good story in search of a character."

"Well, it's like she was dead before she died," Carol-lee says. "She seems so cold to everybody. I mean, her husband is drowning in grief and she just floats away from him without a second thought. And her sons and daughters don't seem to mean much to her at the end. And that whole thing with Robert was so contrived. You really don't need that at all."

I have the sinking feeling all writers must get when they realize they have been fooling themselves. But along with the disappointment is a tiny ray of confidence that I know a little more about the story now. I can see it clearer. Claire needs to be more like someone I know. She needs to be connected to her family, her son, her daughter, her mother. She needs to be more real and alive so her death will be real and her enlightened vision will be real. How will I do this?

"You need to make Claire someone you know," Carol-lee says.

I nod in the way writers do with their best critics.

In unison.

BL

Follow Through

When readers aren't around, writers learn to imagine them. Imagining audiences is one way that writers see beyond their own twitching noses and gain the distance necessary to revise. Here are a few exercises to help connect you with the power of audience.

Write a letter to two very different friends. Write about the same events. Keep both letters and before you mail them, compare. How does your audience affect your voice?

Find an old resume or write a new one for a job you would like to apply for. Take a moment, read over the resume and ask yourself this question: Who am I writing for? Now, just for fun, imagine a new audience: someone you know and love; someone whom you'd tell all the things you didn't include in your job descriptions; someone whom you'll tell, in the words of Paul Harvey, the *rest* of the story.

Freewrite, cluster or brainstorm for five or ten minutes, then compose a new resume out of this new information.

Here is a brief excerpt from mine.

Early Childhood Education

Designed activities and developed curricula for a group of five four-year-olds. Consulted with parents and other care providers at weekly meetings.

Rewrite:

Day Care Survival Worker

Worked with four-year-olds on important social issues like not mashing brownies into the table at snack time, and allowing other members of the group to use the blue cup even though the blue cup is the best.

At weekly meetings tried to convince parents that three-year-olds don't need to know their abc's and Spiderman shirts shouldn't be outlawed, because four-year-olds have to work some things out of their systems lest they become more like the world leaders who appear to emulate them.

Find an insurance policy or some other kind of difficult jargon-filled writing. Take a paragraph and rewrite it for a group of five-year-olds.

Make a list of common objects — forks, plates, lamps, cigarettes. Pick one and describe what it is to the martian who just landed in your backyard. Remember that things are much different on Mars, so be as specific or poetic as possible.

THE LAST DAY

Claire was on her way to the supermarket, but suddenly she had no car, no fingers gripping the steering wheel, no legs and arms, no shopping list. She slipped through the glass doors and floated like smoke up and down the aisles. She had never noticed how beautiful the cans and jars were, stacked so neatly on the shelves; how green was the cellophane grass where the bananas sat heaped in a pile; how the bags of flour puffed out their little chests so proudly. And the people in the supermarket. She could see inside them. She could float past the carts full of beer and Wonderbread into their eyes. It was like stepping through the hard crust of snow to the soft powder beneath or opening a black door

Roland was right. Why not name her right away? "She" seems too coy now.

and being bathed in warm orange light. That old man who looks so sad, whose eyes are storm shutters, the years stretched like old rags over his cheekbones. Look inside and see the young boy running in the summer breeze, a child washed in the clear light of his mother's smile. His breath sweet as candy. His voice a morning lark. They were all prisoners in these bodies, she thought, like the groceries trapped in the clanging steel cages or the food stuffed into the gleaming packages.

I wonder if this is the core of the story (see Day Nineteen) and also what's wrong with it. Claire is trying to figure out what it means to be alive. Maybe she needs to have more figured out already.

She was in the soap aisle when she realized she hadn't bought anything. She couldn't, because she was no longer alive. Dead was the proper term. That word like a hoofbeat pounding on the joy which swelled in her. For a moment she saw the truck swerve into her path. She heard the screech of the tires, the shattering glass, the sirens wailing like lost souls calling her. Then the rising feeling like a large bird spreading its wings inside her chest. What does it mean to die? She had spent most of her life trying to figure out what it meant to be alive.

She looked at the row of detergents. She read the names slowly, one at a time. "JOY, DAWN, AWAKE, YES, CHEER, TIDE, WISK." She read them as though they were prayers which anchored her to this place. If she stopped reading them, she would fly away like a helium balloon on a wave of Muzak, to some place far beyond where nothing would be familiar. "ARISE, ALL, TONE, DIAL, IVORY, EPIC, SUN." She could feel herself going, the supermarket shrinking to the size of a gumdrop on the blacktop beneath. She was going to him. He was calling her.

I still like this. Writer friend Dick Krawiec said in a letter that this section in the supermarket was the best part of the story.

Like a melody, she swept down through the pitched roof of their house on Fairview Avenue. She rolled along the cream colored walls and curled herself around the sofa and the coffee table full of souvenir ashtrays they had bought on their vacation trips together. He was upstairs, sitting on the end of the bed, with the telephone in his hand. The telephone was beeping, and a strange mechanical voice was saying, "IF YOU WISH TO MAKE A CALL, PLEASE HANG UP AND DIAL AGAIN OR PHONE THE OPERATOR FOR DIRECTORY ASSISTANCE." His face was pale and his eyes were red. His shirt was wrinkled and his hair was sticking up in different directions. She stood beside him and felt the tug of his grief like an ocean tide pulling her into the mattress . . .

"Claire," he said. "Please."

"I haven't gone," she said. "I'm here."

He could not hear her, nor could he feel it when she wrapped herself round his shoulders. He was sitting on the bed. He was drowning.

"Please," she said. "Don't mourn me. I'm happy, happier than I've ever been."

He reached for the glass of Scotch on the floor in front of him and chugged it down. Some of it spilled on the bedspread and she contained her desire to get a sponge.

She stood in front of him and looked into his eyes. He was Tom, the man she had lived with all those years, the man whose shirts she'd washed. The man who had helped raise their children. She could never see too deeply into those eyes. There was always something that stopped her, like a wall of lead that closed like a portcullis. Now she could see in there but she didn't want to look. Something held her back; a sense of modesty, perhaps, or was it was fear?

There has to be more here. She seems so cold. She loves Tom in the new story I want to write. Carol-lee was right. Her husband is overcome with grief. She has to feel for him in some way. Still, I like how she won't look into his eyes. What does this really mean? Can I explore this more? What is she really afraid of?

She left him sitting there, the phone still in his hand. She took one last look at the bedroom, beds she had forgot to make, the clothes on the floor she had forgot to bring downstairs, the shoes she had forgot to stick on the rack in the closet. She overcame the urge to put things in order, the sense of embarrassment that people would see her house this way. She melted like butter through the ceiling and drifted into the sky.

It was a feeling of lightness, like being a bubble that could never pop but just drifted here and there in the wind, except it wasn't wind at all. It was something else you couldn't feel but was full of strength and direction, like a thousand voices chanting one steady melody in a low throbbing tone that grew stronger and stronger.

I love this part. I seem to be right on top of the story here, like a surfer riding the crest of a wave.

She looked down and there was the old colonial house with the black shutters. It was summer and the clothesline was full of white sheets. She stood on the gray porch beside her mother, and watched herself sleep as a baby in the bassinet. There were squirrels in the trees chasing branches across the sky, and the sun was beating down on her mother's freckled face.

"I love you, Claire," her mother whispered as she picked the baby up and lifted her to her shoulder against the white cotton dress with the red polka dots.

The image began to flicker like a movie caught in a defec-

I'm not sure about this. I think there needs to be more here. I want this mother to come alive. Is her hair in curlers? Is a Winston dangling from her lips? Does she know what love is?

tive projector. The sun washed away the house and the summer and once again she was drifting.

It was like she was living her whole life at once, a million hearts beating at the same time, a thousand moments competing for her attention. One second it was winter and she was a young girl rolling in the wet snow with Sarah Hawkins, the minister's daughter who lived next door, and taught her how to smoke Winstons. The next minute it was summer and she was at YWCA camp in the mountains, water skiing on the clear blue lake. Then it was winter again and she was in the back seat of the old Dodge, fending off Bob McHenry's moonlight assaults. His slimy Wrigley Spearmint gum lips slid around her face as his hands caressed her with the grace of a boy who spent his evenings bagging groceries.

This doesn't do it for me. Her memories have to be somehow richer and more revealing. Dick wrote me that the scenes in the supermarket are so strong, the rest of the story has to live up to that standard. He's right. This doesn't really cut it. I need to dig a bit here. Claire needs to be someone I know so she can become someone everyone knows.

She was there again, but she wasn't there. She was like dust blown across the landscape of her life and with each moment remembered she could feel herself diminishing, fading into a fabric of fields and houses and sky. She was unraveling, and each strand detached itself and floated away into a pool of clear blue light.

Her children are born, their infant bodies glistening, their bruised eyes staring from some distant closet. They nurse and she feels the warm glow spread through her body. They grow up and go to college. They marry and move away. The moments blend and separate. Tom sits in the chair by the TV set. His eyes are constant. His lips do not move. The football announcer rattles on in the same sing-song. She is in the kitchen doing dishes. She is wiping the yellow Formica counter with a blue sponge, going over the floor with a Johnny mop, going down to the cellar and separating the whites from the lights from the darks. The smell of liquid laundry detergent and bleach burns in her nostrils, floats through her and swirls back into the ground. She is freer now, she is non-stick. She is Teflon.

Again there has to be more here for Claire to come alive on the page. It feels like I'm just skating here.

These mundane memories could probably stay if there was more powerful stuff before them. As it is, they are the most vivid memories she has. This makes Claire like some caricature of an overworked housewife. She could be on a Tide commercial.

It is a green room, and it is autumn. Through the window she can see the maples. A man sits across from her, a young man with chestnut brown eyes that won't stop looking at her. She holds the stem of a lily and slowly shreds the petals.

"I don't understand," the man says.

His name is Robert. A name she has never forgotten.

"I don't love you," she says. "You are my friend, that's all." She doesn't look up at him. In her eyes her mother's fear grows like dead forests. "A boy with no ambition," the voice says.

"But he is a poet," she answers.

"He'll write poems on your grave after you've worked yourself to death supporting him," says her mother.

Robert's eyes keep looking at her. She stares down at the napkin.

"I don't understand," he says.

She doesn't answer. She doesn't look back. She holds the lily by the stem and twirls it in the empty ashtray. She waits for the feeling to go away.

She reads of his death in a motorcycle accident. Her tears drip on the newspaper and smear the gray ink onto her thumb. She washes it in the upstairs sink and continues chopping onions for supper. Tom will notice that her eyes are red and she will tell him about the onions. She will go for a walk after supper. She will see a white lily growing in the shade of a lilac bush. She will not pick it.

The supermarket returns. The pink and blue and yellow detergents run through her, bubble inside her sparkling skin. She is lighter, cleaner. Clear fluorescent light flows through her, scrubbing the faces of the people in the aisle until they open themselves like windows and their lives blow through like spring wind. So much suffering. So much joy. So much sweet confusion tangling itself in these helpless bones. If only they knew the lie of time, the falsehood of footsteps one at a time marching. If only they could be her, just for one moment.

She slides through the checkout line, past the beeping registers. She can remember a loaf of whole grain bread, some toothpaste, a bag of onions. She doesn't know why she remembers this. She laughs at how absurd it is to be dead and to still try to finish the shopping. She will not need groceries anymore, but the others will, and they are still calling her.

It is a sunny day and she is tangled in the branches of an old oak tree. Beneath her, people have gathered. Her daughter Mary has flown in from the coast and Jim has taken the train from Boston. There are bewildered grandchildren and grim-looking faces of her brother Bill and her sister Marjory. The suits are predictable black and the women wear veils. There is a polished mahogany casket with brass handles, and

I cringed every time I read this to myself, but I left it in. "Face it. It's hokey," Carol-lee said. "A poet? C'mon! You don't need it." She's right. It's not that kind of story. It's not about one thing, but a whole life, a whole attitude toward life. I am not James Joyce and this isn't a story about the blind fury of first love. If Robert weren't a poet, it wouldn't be so bad, but why do I need him at all? Women don't need men as much as everybody thinks. There's a story here without Robert. I need to find Claire. Robert will bite the dust in the next revision.

I like this. Isn't this what the story is about, looking through time and space, seeing more than normal people do?

Why does the story get stronger every time I get back to the supermarket? What is it about being dead in a supermarket that is so interesting to me? Maybe we take supermarkets for granted more than any other place on the planet. Maybe the whole story should take place in the supermarket. Interesting.

I want to know more about her relationship with these people.

I feel like I'm going through the motions here. There needs to be more to keep this alive.

This could be developed more. I want to know more about what she really feels about Tom. This is too easy. It doesn't come alive. I don't know her yet.

I want to write more about these relationships. What new insight does she gain from this perspective? Does she see her daughter or son clearer now? Is there something unresolved between them? What?

I like this. Good strong images. It feels right for the story and what I'm trying to say.

a perfectly rectangular hole dug into the clay soil. Two men have dug it. They stand fifty feet away by a marble tomb, drinking Pepsi.

The Reverend is speaking. His voice is clear and loud. He says she was a fine woman who held a warm place in the heart of all the people. He says that she was much loved and will be dearly missed. He says that the Good Lord had taken her and that they have to understand his purpose and accept it. There is a purple sadness in the air. She can almost smell it. A sour, burnt smell, like singed hair. She can feel herself weaving through the people's eyes like a long thread strung with beads.

She tightens like a spring being wound or water spiraling down a drain.

She is above them, looking down on their heads. She can feel the heat rising from their bodies and their thoughts fill her with a rich sadness.

She looks for Tom. He is the closest to the grave, next to her son Jim and Laurie, her daughter. He wears the blue suit that hung in the cedar closet wrapped in plastic. The suit he wore to weddings. She can tell by the way he wavers how many Scotches he had for breakfast. She moves down towards him and watches as he runs his hand over his hair. If she were a pigeon, she knows what she would do. This is her last day. She wants them to laugh. She wants their spirits to soar with hers.

The tears of her daughter burn. She wants to hold her, but there is no longer a shape to her presence and the need dissolves into a feeling of sadness made worse by her son's grimace and her husband's confused stare.

It is almost over. The tug is not as strong anymore. The unraveling nears completion. It grows fuzzy. Their bodies splinter, their heads begin to wash away like sand in an ocean tide. The maples bleach white, the road curls itself into a ball. All vanishes but the white light and the feeling that she is still there, that her life was like a glass of water someone had spilled out and she is now the air inside the glass; weightless but contained.

At first she thinks they were her mother's eyes, then her father's, then her daughter's and her son's. Then, for a moment, they are Robert's eyes, then her own eyes staring from a distant mirror. But they are too big and bright for anybody's eyes. They are the eyes of everyone she had ever known, everyone she has ever seen. All fades and folds itself into these eyes. All vanishes like smoke.

There is a moment when she wonders if she can look into those eyes. Her whole life seems to pull her towards the gathering below. She thinks about laundry piled on the floor in the cellar, garbage that should be put out tomorrow morning, meat that needs to be defrosted. She thinks of moments past, painful moments, frightful moments, moments when she felt alone.

She knows that her whole life has prepared her for this, that nothing is over, that everything will fall from her, and she will still be there rising like a moon over a dark horizon. But soon, even that thought means nothing.

She turns and the eyes bathe her with warm light. The sky grows inside her. There is nothing left to hold her in this world.

I loved the ending and still do. It will be stronger when I can make Claire's life come alive. In a way, death helps her to look into eyes — her own, her family's, and her creator's. But I can't see what she's learned from dying. It's as if she was dead to begin with. I need to make her real so the story says something deeper about human beings and how death connects them with another plane of vision. I need to make Claire live so she can die better.

Day Thirty-Four:
Important Things in Their Place

If you've found readers of your work who make you want to write again, buy them a bottle of Bordeaux. Buy a bottle for yourself. Celebrate. Good readers are hard to find, as are good friends. Let them know that you value them.

Arrange to get together with someone you love to share your work with, but first, try this. Take the draft of an essay or story you've been working on (maybe the one you developed on Day Nineteen), and on a piece of paper write:
- The title
- The first line
- The last line
- The sentence or passage with the most unusual or telling detail
- The most important line

You may have to go out on a limb to choose the key lines in your draft. That's okay. The struggle to decide may help you understand your essay or story better.

When you get together with your reader, give him or her your piece of paper with these five clues about your draft.

Then ask your reader to answer these questions:
- What do you think my essay or story is about?
- What is the tone or the mood?
- What do you think the theme might be? Can you predict what I'm trying to say in this piece?

Then let your reader go ahead and read your draft and talk about how well the title, first line, last line, telling detail, and key passage helped reveal your meaning.

Seeing What You Said

Which of the five fragments of your draft most revealed what you were trying to say? Which misled your reader? Could you find a most important line or was it missing? Was it impossible to choose just one? Is that a problem?

Writer to Writer

The dairy farmer who lives next to Barry in Vermont is a reticent, gentle man—a true Yankee who says more about himself by what he does than what he says. I was talking to Barry about him the other day. I said the man's farm, though weathered and worn, seemed meticulously cared for, almost neat. It impressed me because cows seem to be disorderly creatures, and the old barn and farmhouse appeared to defy the decay that eventually takes everything that is used hard and long.

"It's true," Barry said. "Clarence is a meticulous farmer. Absolutely everything on his farm has its place. You should see his tool shed."

I thought later that, like Clarence, good writers are careful to put important things in their place, where their readers can find them and put them to use. A few days ago, I talked about the importance of making every word count when revising, but that doesn't mean that every word or every paragraph is equally important. A strong piece of writing has a sense of emphasis, partly achieved by *where* in a story or essay you put things. The first and last lines are two places of great importance. So is the title. I struggle with titles. I think most people do. But I also know the struggle is a worthy one, because it is my first opportunity to cue readers to what my piece is about. I realize now that the title for my essay about my father (page 148) is wrong. The piece is not about "The Battle Dad Lost." It's about my own, and the battle is far from over.

At the beginning of this book, Barry and I talked about how specific details bring writing to life, and by now you've had plenty of practice writing with more precision. But some details are more important than others, not only because they are unusual. The strongest details rise from the sea of experience and shed light on the meaning of the story or essay. The clacking of my father's typewriter that used to keep me awake at night reminded me — and my readers — of how bound Dad and I were to the writer's trade. And when his typewriter went silent, the chance to share its joys died. The strongest details have layers like this that reach down into the heart of the draft.

When you did this exercise, you might have had the most difficulty finding the key line. Most essays or stories have one, often embedded in the core paragraph that we talked about on Day Nineteen. Here's mine, from the essay on my father: "It is good, I think, that we live the rest of our lives a little afraid." If I had to choose one sentence the essay could not live without, it would be that one, since it is the most important thing I'm trying to say about being a child of an alcoholic.

Put together, the title, first line, last line, telling detail, and key line should give your readers enough to predict what your piece is about, even without reading it. Think of your drafts like Clarence's tool shed. As you revise, remember that of the many things you have to hang on the walls, some are more important than others. Be careful to put those in the places your readers are likely to find them.

BB

Follow Through

There are other ways to draw a reader's attention to what's important.

- Try isolating your key line — like I did in "The Battle Dad Lost" — in a one-sentence paragraph.
- If you use line breaks (a kind of punctuation where you skip two lines to separate the text into sections), try putting your strongest details in the last line before the break.
- Italics give emphasis, and so do recurrences. Repeat an important line throughout your piece.

See how other writers use the important places in their work, and how they create emphasis. Go to your bookshelf and pull your favorite collection of stories or essays, or pick up a good magazine from your coffee table. Read a slew of first lines, last lines, and titles. Look for other techniques writers use as a cue that they are saying something important.

The Battle Dad Lost

DOVER, N.H. — When I was a child, my father had an office in the room next to my bedroom. It was, it turned out, a temporary office. So much of what my father planned and dreamed and tried seemed temporary or unfinished.

But there was a year that he planned to return to writing full time, planned to write a book and feature pieces for his old employer, the *Chicago Tribune*. On many nights, soon after he put me to bed, Dad would return to his office in his room next door, and I would hear the clacking of his typewriter and smell the smoke from cigarette after cigarette.

I found the sound of the typewriter annoying. It frequently kept me awake and, out of boredom, I would bury my face in my pillow, or under my pillow, and sing. We were both busy composing, my father and I, in adjacent rooms. He would eventually hear my muffled singing, and the typewriter would stop and my door would open a crack.

"Go to sleep, Bruce," he would say gently.

"Stop typing, Dad," I answered, and it made him laugh.

He stopped typing for good some years later and the room next door was converted into a den and the nights went back to silence.

Many years after that, I began to clank away on the same typewriter late at night in a room next to the bedroom, but in another house a long way from the one in Chicago where I grew up. I became a writer, though my father never knew it. He died long before the first few articles were published.

But I still go back to those nights when the typewriter talked and my father tried to keep a few dreams alive. There weren't many years like that. He drank and drank until it dragged him down and finally silenced the typewriter for good.

There was a cult of drinking among the newspaper reporters of the old Chicago school, and some of my strongest memories are of evenings spent with my father at the Boul-Mich, a bar across from Tribune Tower, where chain-smoking reporters in wrinkled shirts would gather every night to tell stories about some politician on the take, or the gruesome results of a local plane crash.

These were drinking stories, and, while I listened, I sat on a barstool next to my Dad and drank bottle after bottle of a soft drink called Squirt. I thought then that, more than anything else, I wanted to grow up to be like those men.

When Dad died, the *Tribune* eulogized the passing of one of its own, a man who for many years worked the city crime beat for the paper and was an occasional feature writer: born to a well-to-do Winnetka family, divorced husband of a well-known Chicago television personality, and survived by two sons.

The obituary didn't say anything about the alcoholism that finally killed him, of course. But I suspect the survivors of the old crew from the Boul-Mich knew, and maybe shook their heads and remembered the old stories Charley would tell over the open mouth of a glass of Scotch.

When Dad died, I remembered those stories and thought them all lies.

That was ten years ago, and in the years that have passed since then I have come to realize that the pain and the torment and the humiliation I felt when my father slipped into hopeless alcoholism did not die with him, as I hoped it would. I have learned to miss him again, especially when I sit down late at night in front of his old Royal typewriter and take up the trade that kept us both awake at night years ago in adjacent rooms.

I have finally forgiven him.

And now I regret that we never had the chance to exchange manuscripts and favorite books, and dreams of bylines in the big magazines. I miss the pride he might have felt if he could read what is written here.

But in another way, a much less predictable way, Dad is still here with me. He is with me every time I drink a glass of wine or Scotch or his favorite vodka and lime, every time I sidle up to a bar to tell a story, and every time I see myself in the mirror and see the same broad forehead, the same dark eyes, the same shadows that framed the face of that young writer in the photographs I keep of Dad during his *Tribune* days.

This is the curse of the sons and daughters of alcoholics. It is the haunting feeling of our own vulnerability to the disease. And we are in danger when we are able to dismiss it simply as a dead ghost of a past we'd just as soon forget.

It is good, I think, that we live the rest of our lives a little afraid.

Maybe it's that fear that has brought me back to this old typewriter, to peck away at painful memories, and to try—through the writing—to understand the loss of a man who could give me a rose bush on my twenty-first birthday, and then drink himself to death before it had a chance to bloom.

Day Thirty-Five:
The Imaginary Friend

Think of a flaw you have. It can be a little thing, like forgetting to close drawers or losing other people's pens or missing appointments. Now, imagine someone much older than you, of the opposite sex. Write for twenty minutes about them, giving them your flaw.

Write quickly.

Seeing What You Said

What part do you like best about your description?
What part seems to come alive? What part doesn't?
Do you want to write more about this character?

Writer to Writer

If a child doesn't like eating broccoli and her mother insists, an imaginary friend might appear and be ordered to eat a heaping bowlful. If a child has a problem cleaning up her toys, an imaginary friend could quickly develop the same problem and promptly be scolded. It's easier to see our own faults in other people, even imaginary people. Perhaps this is why child psychologists spend so much time studying children's doll play.

Novelist Ernest Hebert once described to me a problem he had with a character in a novel that, in his words, just wouldn't come alive. He described the character as a man about his age who worked as a newspaper reporter. Ernie had worked for many years as a reporter. The character was very much like himself. That was the problem. No matter how hard he tried to see him as a separate person, he came across more as a bland observer of other people. I asked him about an older character in another novel who didn't have any trouble coming alive. "I loved writing about him," he said. "He was the father I never had. That was easy."

When we write about other people well, we fill in the gaps of our personalities and our lives. We pump flesh and blood into our longings and fancies. We take ourselves apart and reassemble them in different order, in a different body.

Fiction writers, like young children, don't make up their imaginary friends out of thin air. When you look at what you wrote in this exercise, maybe you begin to see how your imagination gives birth to a new person. I wrote about Flora Quimby, a three-hundred-pound sixty-five-year-old retarded woman who has spent most of her life in a state institution.

At first glance, Flora Quimby is nothing like me, but when I look closer I see certain similarities. Flora wants more out of life than she can ever have. She's been sterilized, but all she wants is a baby. She thinks about it all the time and buys baby clothes. Though people tell her it's impossible, she insists on what she wants against all the odds.

As I think about Flora, I think about my own longing to be a writer. How most of the time I've written despite all the odds, despite all the things people have told me. Though my dream might not be quite as irrational as hers, I've clung to it with the same tenacity. Maybe that's why I enjoy writing about Flora Quimby so much. But I wouldn't feel the same way writing about myself. I'd feel self-important, and because I'd feel that way, I probably wouldn't let as much of me spill onto the page.

Fiction writer Sue Wheeler told me that whenever she felt that her first person narrator was too much like herself, she'd slip the story into third person to gain some distance.

There are certain technical advantages to writing in third person. First person stories are always limited to what the narrator can say. One person is talking and there is nothing the author can do to shut him up. However, in third person, I can reveal characters' thoughts and describe them physically without them stepping in front of a mirror and telling me how they look. I can decide how limited the point of view should be. I can be like Hemingway and focus on the characters' words and actions rather than their thoughts, or I can be impressionistic like Virginia Woolf and stay inside a character's head, listening to every nuance of thought and dream. I can take the godlike stance of Gabriel Garcia Marquez and write about things that will happen years later and years earlier in the same sentence. I can be a camera, or a brain monitor, or a god, or some strange combination of all three.

When we write in the third person, we can fall in love with our characters without those characters falling in love with themselves. We can hover and dive and see through walls and skulls. We can give the kiss of life to a bunch of black marks spread evenly across a page and make a whole person where once there was only white paper.

BL

Follow Through

Go back to your character, or imagine a new one. Continue writing, following some of the suggestions below.

Spend at least two sentences describing your character physically. Make them talk with someone else. Describe something about them or their life that they don't know about.

Example: He was fat and tall. His eyes were like shrivelled peas stuck into the mashed potato of his face.

"Food," he thought. Nora would cook him something greasy and brown. She would do it in the cast iron skillet and the grease would splatter on the white enamel stove.

"Vern," the voice said.

"What?"

It was Nora.

"Eat your carrot stick. You need vitamin A."

"I'm sick of this diet."

"Vern Thompson, you eat that right now."

He bit into the orange substance, but the greasy burgers were already frying in the dark skillet of his heart, and a week from now everyone would know his diet was over.

Think of yourself as a cameraman with an ESP zoom lens. You can go into your characters' heads and float above them. You can see into their lives and beyond to things they know about. You can show them standing there or take a spaceship to the stars and show the planet they are standing on. Have fun!

Here's a few quick exercises to get you seeing the difference between first and third person.

Change popular first person songs into third person. Analyze what happens when Paul McCartney's song becomes "Yesterday/All his troubles seemed so far away . . ." Why are most songs written in the first person?

Write for ten minutes about yourself. Write now as a character in the third person. Use as many of the techniques from above as you can.

Write for ten minutes about an inanimate object in the third person. Bring it to life with words. What is it thinking? Where did it come from? What does it dream of?

Day Thirty-Six: The Thirty-Five Minute Composition

Throughout this book we've talked about the writer's two internal voices: the critic and the child. By now, both have had a chance to exercise their wills. But how well do they work together?

Today, start with another big, unwieldy idea—death—and, using some of the techniques you've experimented with so far, see if in thirty-five minutes you can produce a short composition about it.

1) Cluster the word "death" for seven minutes on a blank page of your journal. Ready? Begin.

2) Spend a minute or two reviewing your cluster. Look for strands or words that will ignite a freewrite. As always, let the words rush to the page. Keep your pen moving. Freewrite for five minutes. Begin.

3) Read your freewrite. Underline lines, passages, or words that surprised you a little, or that you liked, for whatever reason. Now compose a sentence or two that summarizes the most important thing you seem to be saying in your freewrite. This may be hard, but it's important.

4) Freewrite again for five minutes. Begin anywhere. Mark up your freewrite like before, and write another focusing sentence or two. This summary might be like the last one, or totally different.

5) Repeat the process—five-minute freewrite and focusing statement—one more time.

Seeing What You Said

Did your cluster give you a way to anchor the abstract word "death" to your own sea of experience?

Did you have to struggle to generate the three freewrites, or did the words rush to the page each time?

Did your summary sentences build on each other, contradict each other, change what you thought you wanted to say?

Did they help you focus each freewrite? Were they hard to write? Why?

Do you think you have enough sentences to compose a few paragraphs of strong prose?

Writer to Writer

Look at my death cluster on the following page.

At first, I was a little disappointed at what grew here. In the first few branches I seemed to be reviewing worn memories of encounters with death—the time when I struggled to keep pet turtles alive for more than a month, the words my friend spoke at my father's funeral, and the image, blurred by tears, of my first dog's death under the wheel of a milk truck. Another branch, with the words "war," "irony," "beauty," and "horror," seemed to dissipate into vagueness. But I was surprised by a series of words and phrases that brought me back to the ten-year-old Bruce, fascinated by guns and expert at the dramatics of sudden death in my imaginary backyard wars.

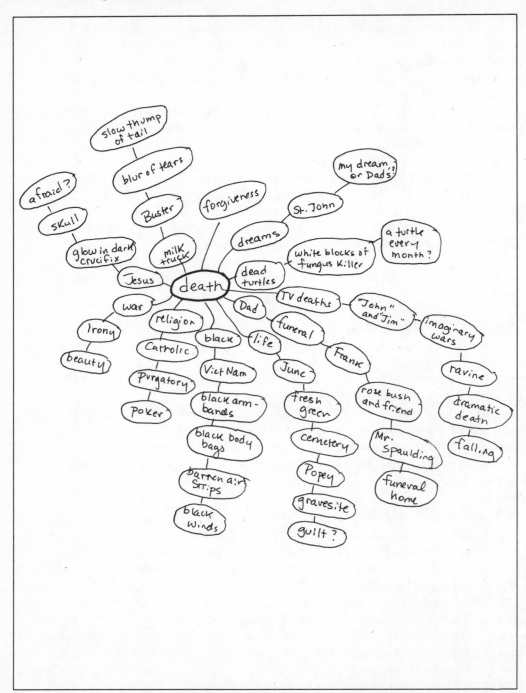

It was that branch that asked to be written about, and here's the freewrite that grew from it:

> I don't remember how many times I died in imaginary wars when I was a kid. I think it wasn't more than twice a day. Somehow it didn't seem right to die more than that, and I'm not sure I could summon up the dramatics to die more often than that. I used to "play" army often, with my good friend Chris Field, in the lush, winding ravines that threaded their way through the backs of the houses of my neighborhood. All the ravines had water in the bottom of them — not much, just enough to give the hint of a stream. There was an old wooden bridge that spanned the ravine from the back of a neighbor's house, and it seemed that the enemy (usually imaginary Germans) took a particular interest in blowing it up. I was its protector — a GI named Jim (I don't know why I liked that name so much; surely it wasn't because of Jimmy Olson on the Superman TV show — my favorite program — who was too naive to make a good soldier), and I remember dying often on behalf of that bridge, taking a shot in the chest, clutching it, and tumbling down the ravine with the loose dirt falling with me. I thought I was pretty good at dying. I borrowed all my images of it from movies and television, and it had dramatic meaning. I often uttered last words to my friend Chris, who hovered above me, occasionally cradling my head in his arms. I wish I could remember what I said. I'm not sure whether my frequent death prepared — or ill-prepared — me for understanding what it meant. I know it didn't help me understand what real war was about. I learned that from television when I was a little older, watching with awe as rows of black body bags were neatly lined up on some barren airstrip in Vietnam. The wind was always blowing.
>
> I liked dying. So did Chris. I think he died more than I did, and I think he was better at it. A better actor. His name was always John.

I liked this freewrite because it helped me remember how much I liked to die, and that surprises me now, and makes me wonder why. I want to pick up on that in the second freewrite. I also liked some of the specifics about the ravine behind my house, especially the wooden bridge, which I defended with such seriousness back then.

Here's my summary:

> I first came to understand death through play, as a casualty in imaginary backyard wars. I liked dying.

Freewrite two:

I'm not exactly sure why I liked dying. I suppose the dramatics were a part of it. Clutching my chest, falling to the ground, rolling down, dangerously limp, to my final resting place. Death seemed pretty benign, even glorious.

I guess watching TV deaths took the fear out of it. It was also a chance to say profound, meaningful things—a dying soldier always speaks from his heart. Maybe that's it. When I watched TV, the only time the soldiers would confess their true feelings was with a belly full of shrapnel, while their comrades—like lovers—hovered over them. How strange.

I was with a young friend named Conal the other day. He's three. And he loves killing people. As a matter of fact, he killed me repeatedly with a machine gun mounted on a tractor at my house, killed me while I was trying to dig a hole to plant a birch tree. My imaginary grave. I clutched my chest (it all came back) and dropped a few times, but every time I would magically revive myself, Conal would shoot me again and I would feel obliged to die dramatically once more. It was tiring to die. The kid was ruthless. Killing me may have been the only time he seemed to have control over an adult, which, strangely, is what real killing is all about—control, ultimate control.

I didn't learn much from the first half of this freewrite, but the stuff about my three-year-old pal Conal, and his delight in repeatedly gunning me down, helped me to understand how a child would enjoy imaginary murder. My summary:

Children can be ruthless killers of imaginary enemies—especially if they're adults. What power to see a grown man fall into a ditch, using nothing more than a pointed finger and a mouthful of saliva.

Freewrite three:

I had a fascination with guns as a kid, though somewhere along the line it turned into disinterest and finally distaste. I used sticks (short ones were machine guns, long ones rifles—a good pistol was hard to find [perhaps wisely, nature doesn't seem inclined to produce many good stick pistols]). Occasionally I would latch onto a store-bought gun, usually a water pistol or a western cap gun with a holster. The ammunition came in long red paper spools with dots of powder. I always thought if I could scratch enough powder from the cap strips, I could make a really powerful explosive, but I never had the patience to try. I would carry my guns into battle in the backyard, or I would shoot the dog. There was little satisfaction in that, because he cowered and it made me feel bad.

There was a strange kind of magic in the act of pointing a gun at someone or something. Maybe that was the part of it that had more to do with using real guns than imaginary ones. I absolutely loved seeing my friend Chris fall from a well-placed bullet.

We used to have a .22 rifle in our basement. It was a primitive weapon — probably dangerously poorly cared for — with a barely finished hardwood stock and a rusting steel barrel. Like most boys, I was fascinated by it, and I used to finger the bolt, clicking it in and out, reveling in the sound. Fortunately, I was never tempted to use it in my backyard skirmishes with the Axis. I preferred sticks or borrowed toy rifles. I shot the .22 on several occasions at a small target pinned to a box full of newspapers. I was a poor shot, and though I enjoyed trying to hit the target, the rifle's report was so loud it made my ears ring. It didn't occur to me then that that might mean I wasn't cut out to be a soldier.

Less happened in this freewrite than the first two. I do like the specifics on the red paper caps that used to arm my toy pistol, though I'm not sure how I can use that information. I also see the writing here building on the idea I discovered earlier, embodied in this final focusing statement:

The power imaginary guns offer a child is a lot like the power real ones offer adults — a chance to exercise their will over something or someone else. In my own dream world my shot was straight and true, and death was swift and dramatic, which is why I preferred a long stick to a rusting .22, and took aim at my best friend instead of the bullseye of a cardboard target.

BB

Follow Through

At some point, everyone thinks about or deals with death. It's a theme that often finds its way into our writing. (Remember Barry's dead woman, Claire, coming to life again in the draft of his short story on Days Fifteen and Twenty?) Because it is such a universal subject, death is especially difficult to write about well. What can we bring to it that hasn't already been said before? When I began this exercise, I wasn't at all certain that I had much new to add. I still don't think I'm saying anything particularly profound, but I am pleased with the angle I found to talk about it. Unless my cluster had suggested it, I doubt it would have occurred to me to write about my lust for killing and dying in backyard battles. In each freewrite, I allowed the words to rush to the page uncensored, and remembered something surprising — the day a three-year-old riddled me with bullets in my backyard, my defense of a besieged wooden bridge, and the ambivalence with which I handled an old .22.

I let my internal critic have a go at it, too. Between each freewrite, I sorted through the chaos of information, leading me to a notion of what I was trying to say. Subtly, it began to help me shape the material, until now I feel ready to compose a short essay, using what I've learned through the writing.

It is this negotiation between the two voices in your head — the child who looks and remembers with wonder and openness, and the critic who wants to know "so what?" — that will give your prose power. We've talked about this often here. In the beginning, we urged you to free that childlike voice from the clutches of criticism through techniques like freewriting and clustering. Later exercises coached your internal critic on aspects of craft. As you near the end of *Discovering the Writer Within*, invite both to the page with all the freedom and knowledge they've gained, and marvel at the powerful things they can do together.

Take ten minutes to compose a three- or four-paragraph essay based on the work you did in the first half of this exercise. Here's mine. It needs more work, but I like what I've started to do with it.

The Ruthlessness of Children with Imaginary Guns

I was digging a hole to plant a birch tree the other day, when my three-year-old friend Conal came by to kill me. He shot me repeatedly in the chest from across a field, where he discovered an imaginary gun mounted on a John Deere tractor. I remembered how to die, and with each well-aimed shot I clutched my chest, spun once, and fell to the dirt. Conal squealed with sadistic delight every time.

After the fifth fall, I brushed myself off and resumed digging the tree hole. I thought about the ruthlessness of children with imaginary guns, remembering my own joy as a child when I found branches from old oaks that were transformed into rifles and machine guns. I loved to kill my best friend Chris Field, but even more, I loved to die. With a grimace and a gasp, I would utter my last words, cradled in Chris's arms, only to revive minutes later and give him the chance to also fall gloriously.

My youthful fascination with guns did not seem to transfer to the real thing. We had a rusting .22 rifle in our basement, and though I used to love clicking the bolt in and out, reveling in the sound, I didn't long to fire it. I preferred sticks. They had the same effect without the loud report. And in my imaginary world my shot was true, and my victim's death always dramatic.

Conal took aim once more from across the field and I prepared to die. I realized later that his enthusiasm for killing—and my own as a child—was similar to those who grow up to love real guns. They are a tool to control. What power to see a grown man fall into a tree hole, using nothing more than a pointed finger and a mouthful of saliva.

Day Thirty-Seven:
The Page Is a Frypan

Yesterday Bruce talked about uniting the child and critic in your writing. The same two voices follow you from the writing desk and into the world. Writers embrace and scrutinize potential subjects with the same zeal as they do the ones they choose to write about. Ideas ripen like fruit in dark closets. And, of course, just as often they rot. This exercise takes you to the marketplace to squeeze the melons.

Look through newspapers and magazines searching for one sentence that fascinates you. I find a tabloid like the *Weekly World News* works well. Headlines like, "Scientists Say Dinosaurs Honked Like Buicks," or "Huge Space Sheep Seen in Brazil," or "Ancient Romans Stop a Busload of Tourists in Morocco," make me want to write. But maybe you want to try regular front page headlines like "First Lady Meets with Astrologer to Decide Fate of the Nation," or "Grain Prices Soar as Drought Scorches Midwest," or, from the sports page, "Cardinals Maul Giants" or "Tigers Destroy White Sox." Or take a walk to the local movie theater like I did yesterday and copy the marquees:

Three Men and a Baby
Unbearable Lightness of Being
Above the Law

Collect five provocative sentences, then choose the one that wants most to be written about. Next, go for a walk or do some errands, but take your journal with you. Search for something to write about. Look at people, places, activities. Go to a diner and eavesdrop a few lines or turn on the TV and copy some dialogue. If you're stuck, try remembering stories your parents told you. (See sidebar.) Freewrite, or go to their house and interview them. Choose five short sentences from all your freewriting. Pick the best one.

Put each sentence at the top of a blank page and write two quick, bad poems using your sentences as the first lines. Write fast. Let the bad poems grow branches that can be lopped off later. If you have trouble writing, remember that you must write a bad poem. You mustn't be Shakespeare or Emily Dickinson or Robert Frost. There are too many immortals cluttering up the world's libraries. The world needs more disposable poets.

Here is my bad poem about the headline I found in the *Weekly World News*.

> **World Police Hunt for the Man Who Kills with His Mind**
> *He was last seen*
> *murdering an egg salad sandwich*
> *which gave him indigestion.*
> *His therapist*
> *told him to think*
> *positive, nice thoughts*
> *and all his friends might stop dying.*
> *"Life is murder," he said.*
> *"I love you," said the therapist.*
> *The man stood up*
> *and his chair died*
> *then the carpet rolled up and died*
> *and the door died when he opened it.*
> *"Please," the therapist said*
> *as his polished desk*
> *gasped, and his*
> *couch curled up into*
> *a ball.*

Seeing What You Said

Did your poem grow quickly from the sentence, or did you have to struggle to string words together? Did you let yourself run with the idea, or did your sentence seem less fertile once you began writing the poem?

Can you think of other places to look for poems?

Writer to Writer

I once had dinner with poet Charles Simic and a few students from our poetry workshop. We would be talking, and all of the sudden Charley would ask for a napkin, scribble down something, and stuff it in his pocket. He said it was a note to himself that he would write in his notebook later. He had an almost guilty look on his face, and it was clear this was a man who never stops writing poetry, not even to eat pizza.

Poets are pack rats. They are never too busy to step out of the water to scribble a few lines to themselves. They know that poems and stories are embedded in the clay of everyday life, and only a keen eye or a well-tuned ear can dislodge them.

In a book of Buddhist scriptures, I once found an unusual story about a Bodisatva who fed himself to a hungry tigress. One line in the story stuck with me. After the Bodisatva died, the writer said, "He continued to live on in a unique way by virtue of a divine psychic power." I read the line several times, and each time I got a tickling sensation in my chest. I felt I could understand exactly what it meant but at the same time it was a total mystery. The next day I wrote a poem about it.

Here it is.

Old Love
He continued to live on in a unique way
by virtue of a divine psychic power.

She sees him
on the front page of the newspaper:

MAN DIES
BUT CONTINUES TO LIVE ON
IN A UNIQUE WAY
BY VIRTUE OF A DIVINE
PSYCHIC POWER;
SCIENTISTS BAFFLED.

That night,
he comes to her
all pink and purple,
a hissing shadow
beneath the thick blanket.

You continue to live on in a unique way,
she says.
By virtue of a divine psychic power,
he replies.

Divine my ass
can't even die properly,
follow something to the end
for ONCE in your life!
Don't sulk now.

Not sulking,
just continuing to live on
in a unique way.

She thinks of days past
when he wasn't so unique
when divine psychic power
was not an issue,
when together,
they continued to live
on and on.

I don't really like the poem anymore. It seems unnecessarily glib, especially compared to that first feeling I had when I came across that line. But when I look now at the story I am writing about Claire, I realize I am still writing about that feeling and I can see some of the same elements from the poem in the story. I had forgotten about the poem until now, but my unconscious never forgets.

Ted Walker, the English poet, used to make an analogy between writing and cricket. He said that as a boy he always felt he got better at cricket over the winter by watching it on TV. He would step out onto the field on the first day of spring and be able to do things with the bat he couldn't do the year before. His unconscious had been working all winter while camped in front of the tube. In a similar way, ideas ripen in the back corners of the mind. A quick poem or a few lines to yourself is a way of preserving a flash of inspiration for the day when you can write it.

I was listening to a sociologist on National Public Radio shortly after the crash of the space shuttle. He was describing the crash's effect on the thousands of children who watched it on TV. "The children have to learn that their grief is normal," he said. I was frying onions at the time. There is a grease stain on the page in my journal where I wrote down his words and a few notes to myself. The onions burned in the frypan, but two months later the poem had boiled itself down on the page.

Unsentimental Education
Tell them
not to throw snowballs
at the granite tombs
or wipe their sniffly noses
on Santa's sleeve,

and those sweet dreams,
they musn't eat them
before they've had their supper.

Tell them that
their grief is normal

before you pack
their lunchboxes with
biscuits and bones
and an apple
full of worms
with the teacher's name on it.

BL

Follow Through

Take your poem and play with it again. Trim it back or let it grow more. Chase down a new idea or hone an old one. Listen to your child and your critic sing in harmony.

Here are a few ideas to help trigger poems or stories. Try one or two when inspiration is running dry.

Find a place that evokes a strong feeling, either positive or negative. Go there with your journal and write down details. Write a descriptive poem of the place without revealing your feelings directly.

Take an abstract concept, like work or marriage. Write twenty lines about it on a blank page in your notebook. Next, use your lines to write a poem with the concept word repeating every so many lines. Example:

> *Marriage*
> *communicate*
> *not walking away*
> *Divorce*
>
> *Marriage*
>
> *Having our first baby*
> *paying bills*
> *What was I like before?*
>
> *Marriage . . .*

Pretend you are a Japanese poetry master. Sketch the world you live in with short poems like haiku (but don't count syllables). Put on your kimono and head to the shopping mall with pen and journal in hand. Dash off poems like,

> *I see my reflection*
> *in the eyes*
> *of a plastic Easter bunny*
> *at K-mart.*

Write poems about the objects in your room. Give them a voice. Let them talk about you. Rewrite the world with one sentence, then follow it. Have fun (see Day Twenty-Nine). Think of yourself as Harold with your purple crayon. If you are lost in the ocean, draw yourself a boat. Don't be afraid to change the shape of things. Look at these examples; then go crazy.

> *Lee Harvey Oswald does not shoot President Kennedy.*
> *He takes an Aerobics class instead.*
> *He decides it's better exercise,*
> *a smarter career choice.*

Or this one:

> *A man*
> *who was afraid of his own shadow*
> *decided to bury it in the white sand along a beach.*
> *But the shadow proved difficult*
> *and buried the man instead.*

Think of a moment in childhood and write a quick poem about it, somehow drawing on all your acquired wisdom since (see Day Twelve, and the poem "Starlight").

Make a list of objects and pick the most unlikely one to write a poem about. Then, write the poem like this one from my ex-student Meghan Just, a.k.a Stephen Lewis:

> **Ode to a Head of Cauliflower**
> *White bunched, cradled in farmer's fingers,*
> *Sitting in green glorious stems, it lingers*
> *A message mute, a gift for sages.*
> *The cauliflower endures, a flavor for the ages.*
>
> *So quickly set your pot upon the stove.*
> *Turn the burner high, a clothespin on your nose.*
> *Each nostril knows this ain't no rose.*
> *The poet knows he better stick to prose.*

My Father's Stories

Every storyteller is indebted to the first stories they were told as children. To some, they were fairy tales or Dr. Seuss books; to others, old stories about real people who lived in real houses and cities. The first stories stick with you and sprout voices inside your head. They are a reservoir of inspiration for years to come. Remembering the first stories can be a way of reconnecting with the inner voice which buzzes in your jaw when you sit at the typewriter and pound at the keys.

My father's stories were about growing up poor and Jewish on the Lower East Side of Manhattan. He would tell them to my brother Michael and me at bedtime when we burrowed in the clean sheets. There were little potatoes called "mickies." They'd roast them with newspapers in rusty old milk cans. He had a friend named Howie who cheated at Monopoly and a stray dog named Pal that he fed leftover ice cream from the garbage at the candy store.

When I try to write my father's stories, they seem flat and uninteresting, a bunch of words scattered on the page. Yet I know they were much more than that when I first heard them. Why else would they have stuck with me all these years?

I see my father sitting at my bedside. He pulls the covers around me and the stubble of his beard scrapes my cheek as he gives me a goodnight kiss. "I'm going to tell you a story," he says, and rubs his palms together in anticipation.

My eyes fight off sleep. My head avoids the pillow's soft caress.

"When I was a young boy, about your age, growing up on the Lower East Side, we were very poor. We had no money."

The wind knocks at the window, and Michael and I snuggle deeper into the sound of his voice.

"The neighbors, they would bring us food. Little potatoes. We'd cook them with newspaper in a milk can. We'd call them mickies.

"One day I was very hungry and there were no mickies to eat. I couldn't sleep all that week because my stomach grumbled so much. I made up my mind. I was going to steal a pie from the local candy store, a little Table Talk Pie. A pineapple pie.

"I walked to the back of the store and waited until no one was looking. Then I slid the pie under my shirt, but when I looked up, I saw Mr. Greenbaum's eyes in the reflection of the glass showcase. Mr. Greenbaum was a big man who never seemed to smile. His son had died and his wife was very sick. Many times I'd seen him yell at the children not to play stickball in front of his store. He said he would break their necks if he caught them again.

"I didn't know what to do. If I put the pie back, he'd see me and know that I was stealing it. If I kept it, he would call the police and I would go to jail. I wondered if they would feed you pie in jail. I walked slowly toward the front of the store. I was seven years old. I was hungry. I didn't know any better. Each step seemed like a hundred years: past the penny candy jars, the baseball cards, the chewing gum, the ice cream freezer. Past all the things my stomach longed for.

"When I got to the register I didn't look up, but I knew he was standing there, waiting. I reached for the metal doorknob and heard his voice.

'Boy.'

"My heart beat like a big drum. My fingers froze to the knob. I thought about running. I thought about crying. I thought about not getting to eat the pie and my stomach grumbling all night.

'Boy,' he said again.

"I looked at him. First at his big belly, then the red suspenders, then the little white buttons on his shirt. Then I looked at his face, and there was a smile growing at the corners of his lips.

'Goodbye,' was all he said.

"You see, he didn't have the heart to take the pie from me. I was so skinny. He took pity on me and looked the other way.

"That night I saved the pie till almost bedtime. It was pineapple, and when I bit into it, the crust flaked onto the pillow and some filling dripped down my chin. My stomach stopped grumbling, and when I put my head on the pillow and closed my eyes, the last thing I thought of was the storekeeper's smile."

The drowsiness overcame us. The night was now a warm cloak around our shoulders. I remember my father pulling the covers tighter, and another kiss on the forehead. I remember feeling so well cared for, so well fed.

My father just retired from the job he worked for thirty-seven years. Sometimes when I visit my mother and him, they want to know how I got to be a writer. "Where did you get such stories?" my mother asks.

My father sits in his chair in the living room reading his newspaper. All around him are the signs of his successful journey from the ghettos of Manhattan.

"Daddy, you told us stories," I say. "You showed me what a story was. Remember your dog Pal, the mickies, that time you stole the pie and the man looked the other way?"

My father looks up. The paper drops to his lap. For a moment I see in his eyes all the pain, all the joy. Stories begin and end in those eyes. Children wait for big hands to lift them into the sky.

"You're such a writer," he says and picks up his newspaper again.

Day Thirty-Eight:
From Failure to Faith

Until yesterday, you may have never written a poem. Well, maybe when you were eight, on Valentine's Day. You asked Ruth to marry you and run away to live in an abandoned house in the woods behind the Burman's house. You promised to bring a cardboard suitcase full of white bread and candy, and a plastic ring with a glass diamond.

That poem doesn't count, you think. You're not a poet. You're not a novelist. You're not a painter, a photographer, an essayist, a sculptor. You're not an artist. You look at the work in the pages of your journal—thirty-seven days' worth of work—and you wonder: "What is it that I've really accomplished?"

Here's one way to find out: paint. Get yourself some watercolors—the cheap kind that you brought to school in second grade, with eight rectangles of basic colors neatly lined up in a plastic case. Get a glass of water and a rag to clean your brush. Turn to a blank page in your journal and fill it with color. Paint anything: yourself, the view out your window, your writing desk, a watermelon, the meadow you and your collie used to play in on hot August days. Or just play with the colors, see how they mingle and merge and take on new identities. Fill another page with your watercolor experiments if you'd like; then set aside five minutes to freewrite in your journal about what it was like to put down the pen and pick up a paintbrush, and play.

Seeing What You Said

Was this fun, or did you keep saying to yourself—"I'm no painter"—and vow never to show anyone your painted pages? Did anything surprise you?

Writer to Writer

Two friends from Montana visited the other day, and they asked me about this book, now almost completed. I told them that I thought it was a good book, but that I wasn't sure. I am never sure about anything I've ever written, and I wonder if it will always be that way.

"You're a real writer now," Charlie said. "That's great."

"He even has a card," my wife Karen said. "Do you have one of your business cards with you? They say, 'Bruce Ballenger, Writer.' "

I sheepishly pulled out one of the cards from my wallet, one of the few times I've ever done that, and passed it around.

"That's great," Charlie said.

Though he said it with sincerity, I felt like I did when my mother framed a finger painting I made in the first grade. It had a background of confused red squiggles, topped with large flowers drawn in colored chalk. Mom thought it was wonderfully creative, and she hung it in the stairwell going up to the third floor of our old house.

I never had the heart to tell her that the girl sitting next to me in class drew those flowers, that my only contribution was the red swirls of paint. Every time I passed that framed example of my early artistry, I turned away with guilt. It reminded me I was a faker, a fraud. The flowers made that picture, and they weren't mine.

I feel that way about writing, too. Though the words on these pages are mine, I can't help but feel sometimes that I'm pretending to be a writer, in the same way I pretended to be an artist with finger paints and chalk many years ago. I keep waiting to be found out.

I may, in part, have had those business cards printed to convince myself that I am a writer after all. Like most people, I want to be taken seriously. My own self-doubts make that hard to pull off sometimes, and afraid of risk.

Many days ago, Barry spoke of the demons of doubt, those internal terrorists out to sabotage our good feelings about our work by reminding us of our failures. Unlike our internal critics, who usually want us to do better, the demons of doubt hope to prevent us from even trying.

I hadn't picked up paints or drawing paper since I became an adult, because I was convinced that my hand would once again betray my lack of talent. I have met many people, including successful writers, who felt the same way. When you first wet your brush to begin this workout, you may have confronted your own demons, determined to convince you that painting has no place in a writing book, and you have nothing to gain from even crude experiments with color. You may not have even bothered to try.

But if you dug up that old plastic case of watercolors and took the brush to the page with a sense of joy and delight and wonder, then you have probably learned one of the most important things any artist could learn — to believe in yourself. A willingness to openly and enthusiastically try things that you think you cannot do well — like painting, or poetry, or prose writing — is an act of faith.

It is still not something that comes easily to me. I had to force myself to pick up a brush again and begin tentatively painting the hill and the pine tree outside my window. Before long, I was experimenting with blends of color — yellow and green and brown — trying to capture the tint of the spring grass in the field. It was all awkward and new, but when I was done, I felt strangely happy. How could something so poorly done give me such satisfaction, I wondered?

Because I tried.

It seems so simple, so obvious. But this exercise helped remind me again that writers or painters — or plumbers, for that matter — are not born, but *shaped by failures that they grow to see as experiments instead*. This is a book of experiments. See each journal entry as an attempt to get at something that may or may not make you a better writer. If you've made it this far, what you've accomplished may not be a publishable essay or short story. What you've ac-

complished is the will and the discipline to keep at it, and the faith that if you
do, you won't need business cards to remind you that you're a writer. You
already are.

BB

Follow Through

Experiment with something else you never thought you could do. If you
skipped over the photography exercise on Day Eight because you thought you
couldn't take a creative picture if your life depended on it, risk your life and
take some.

Circle back to other exercises in this book that you were sure you couldn't
do. Give those a shot, too.

Day Thirty-Nine:
Does It Have to End This Way?

Think for a minute about your life. Write "My Life" in the center of a cluster
diagram and play with different aspects. Your job. Your family. Your leisure
activities. Think about all the different things you do and all the things that
make you who you are. Make a list.

Now, I know it's something you don't like to think about, but at the risk of
sounding like a life insurance salesman, I want you to imagine your death.
How old are you? Where are you? What does it feel like? What do you think
about?

I know, you are saying to yourself, "This is morbid. This is depressing. This
is stupid. I can't do this." Stop.

Think of yourself as a child, practicing death scenes on the living room rug.
Remember the drama, the wonderful pathos. Play with your death like a rubber
ball. Bounce it around on the page.

Try to make your death personal. Make it grow out of some aspect of your life. If you love to ski, die in a skiing accident. If you sleep soundly at night, die in your sleep in the middle of some dream.

Use your imagination, but make your death real. Make it personal. Create that final moment with as much detail as you can.

Freewrite, brainstorm, or cluster. Then take twenty minutes and write a description of your death.

Seeing What You Said

Was it difficult to write about your death? Why? Does your death seem to grow directly out of your life, or did you write it without thinking about who you are?

Was this exercise fun or morbid? Could you write about some other person's death more easily?

What does your death say about the way you lived your life? What did it feel like to write about your death?

Writer to Writer

Henry the Eighth died of syphilis, Marilyn Monroe of an overdose of barbiturates. Ghandi was shot, and so were Lee Harvey Oswald, Martin Luther King, Jr., and Billy the Kid. John Keats, the Romantic poet, died of tuberculosis before his twenty-third birthday. Virginia Woolf filled her pockets with stones and walked into a river. People's deaths define their lives. Death is like the period at the end of the sentence. It is emphatic and holds everything that comes before it. Death is the ultimate ending, and like all endings, if it's strong it tells us a great deal about what went before it.

I have a problem with endings in both my writing and my life. I hate to say goodbye, I forget to close drawers, I leave silverware in the sink after I've washed all the dishes, I leave the last dribs of milk in the gallon jug for someone else to finish.

When it affects my writing, I turn to my corkboard. Gustave Flaubert said, "A work of art is never finished. It's only abandoned." Unfortunately, the same doesn't apply to the rusty garden tools I forgot to put away and the laundry that lies unfolded on the rug upstairs. Life is about doing things to the end—otherwise you end up with frayed ends. I have a file full of aborted short stories that have followed me around for years like lost children. Of course I will finish them someday. Someday is the operative word.

Even as I write I think, I should have let Bruce write this day. His personality is more conducive to finishing things. I'm a beginning sort of guy. I'm great at finding ideas, getting them on the page, falling in love with them and nurturing them along. But when it comes time to finish a story, I get this uncomfortable queasy feeling, like I am being asked to put a lid on a bottle of foaming Coke.

I write a quick ending, and it's usually bad. It is too pat or easy and it weakens the story. So I write another one, and it's a little better. Then I write another two or three, and they're all maybe a little better, but none of them really satisfies me. So I reread the story and I think about it and I write some great endings. The kind where you say to yourself, "Move over, James Joyce, here I come." These are, of course, the worst of all, and I eventually collapse in despair and settle for an earlier, more benign ending.

As a writing teacher, I'm great at giving advice about endings to students. I say, "Don't write endings, discover them." Look at what you've written and find the place where the end seems natural. End it there with a sentence or two. Don't summarize. As novelist Tom Williams said to me, "Endings are like footballs. Readers take them and run with them." It weakens a story if the reader knows what it's about totally. You need to leave a lot up to the reader's imagination, but not too much.

Brilliant advice. If only I could follow it. It's just not that simple. Every story, every essay, every book is different, just as every life is. Maybe in this exercise you had yourself jump off a cliff, or you drowned in the Black Sea on a summer vacation. Maybe your death was long and painful, or maybe you died suddenly by a gunshot wound from a jealous lover or in the middle of dreaming that you were playing Aida in Verdi's opera. Maybe your description will help you understand something about your life. You might make the connection that your written endings should be about the core of your story or essay, not something tacked on at the end. A good ending may be surprising, but it is *always* inevitable.

Ernest Hemingway said that every story worth reading was about death. There is no drama, no conflict, no inspiration without the impending sense that all is temporary. There is also no laughter and no heroism. Yet some writers avoid death's influence. They write happy endings to sad stories. They clean things up for their readers or themselves. It's a natural impulse to avoid unpleasant things or to keep a favorite character alive, even when you know it's a better story if he or she dies. If you write an essay which opens a can of worms you are not willing to explore, your ending might close the discussion and comfort the reader, instead of challenging him to think. If you watch TV, you know all about these sentimental endings. How many TV shows leave you with something unresolved to think about? How many do you remember?

I'm not saying that you must always write unhappy endings, only that your endings must always be true to the events which precede them. Fiction writer Carolyn Chute, whose stories about down-and-out rural folk often end tragically, has a sign above her typewriter which speaks to the wish we've all had since we heard our first fairy tale: MORE HAPPY ENDINGS. Writers can try to make things turn out okay, but their stories don't always cooperate.

Ever since we began writing this book, I've thought about how I would end my portion. Yet now that I'm here, there is nothing I can say about writing which will tie things up neatly. That's not what endings should do anyhow. Right? So let me just tell you about my death, because it's late at night and I should be doing my laundry.

I am old and I sit at a wooden desk writing in my journal. It is winter and I am writing about a tropical paradise where lemons and oranges grow on lush green trees.

I stop writing and walk to the window and stare at the snow-covered field. An old pain in my chest spreads through my limbs like fire. I stumble back to the desk and see that my journal has become a large open window.

I fall through it, into the land I was writing about. The jungle is a rainbow of lush colors. I taste the sweet fruit. Jasmine flowers fill me with sweet fragrance.

Then a voice calls from above. It's a familiar voice, my wife's voice. She tells me I forgot to imagine all the laundry that still needs to be folded and put away. Did I think I could get out of this world that easy?

Suddenly the jungle vines turn into BVD's and nightgowns, stockings and bras.

I look up to see the window I fell through, but it's gone. I grab my machete but it's turned into my notebook. I sit down on a stump and begin to write:

"The man folded and put away the jungle. Then he went to bed."

BL

Follow Through

Here are a few more exercises to help connect you with the power and complexity of endings. Pick one or two and see where they take you.

Write an ending to a piece you haven't written yet. Look at it. Then write another ending to the same piece.

Rewrite the endings to TV shows to make them more realistic. Don't be afraid to put detectives in the hospital or send Lassie to the vet. Realize that life cannot be broken down into half-hour segments.

If you are a soap opera fan, try this one. Take the different characters in the soap and write one conclusive paragraph about the rest of their lives. Example: Derek marries Claudia, gives up medicine and becomes a tuna fisherman in Florida. They have three children, none legitimate, and they spend their old age recounting love affairs between games of shuffleboard.

Make your epilogues as believable as you can from the facts about each character.

Write the end of a novel, a short story, and an essay.

Rewrite the ends of fairy tales to make them real for you (see Day Twenty-One).

Read the first page of a short story and try to predict the ending. Then find another story, read the last page, and try to predict the beginning. Notice the close relationship between beginnings and endings. Try interchanging them in your own work and see what happens (see Day Thirty-Four).

Day Forty: A Writer's Welcome Signs

Today we'll end where we began forty days ago. Freewrite for seven minutes, beginning with these four words:

When I write, I . . .

Begin.

Return to what you wrote on Day One. Compare both freewrites. Now make a list of things that have changed about the way you write. Celebrate the progress you've made—even if it seems modest—by going to your favorite restaurant and ordering something really sinful, maybe something with chocolate as thick as a Greenland glacier, or a cheap hot dog smothered with yellow mustard and pickles. Eat it joyfully. Walk calmly and confidently out the door and down the block, then do a little dance on the curb. You're a writer.

Seeing What You Said

For a change, don't pay attention to what you've said. *See how much you have to say*. Flip through the pages in your journal.

Love your good writing, love your bad writing, love yourself because you wrote at all.

Writer to Writer

A few years back when I married Karen, we honeymooned on St. John in the U.S. Virgin Islands. It is beautiful there, but also significant to me, since my Dad's ashes are scattered around a large basalt boulder on one of the island's highest mountains. Dad would often pull out a wrinkled postcard of the mountain and the bay below. "That's where I'm going to live someday," he said to anyone who would listen. "That's where I'm going to live and that's where I'm going to die."

Like many of his dreams, this one slipped away. It lodged for a while in my own heart, close to another longing my father unknowingly passed on to me. We both wanted to be writers.

This is a dream I probably share with you, too, especially if you've traveled these forty days with Barry and me. It doesn't matter whether you took our advice, or faithfully attempted every exercise we proposed. What matters is that you wrote, every day, whatever came from your heart and mind. Writers aren't writers because there are bookstores with shelves and magazine racks to hold the fruit of their work. Writers are writers because they write, whether they're published or not.

Unfortunately, that was not what my father believed. When he finished the manuscript for his first book, only to learn that his publisher's new owners would not honor his contract, he gave up and never wrote much again. He talked a lot about writing, as many people do, but when he stopped parking himself in front of the desk and typewriter, he stopped being a writer.

Writing is work. That's not news, which is partly why throughout this book Barry and I have tried to help you discover writing's reward—the feast of surprises that await you as your words make it to the page. Most writers learn to hunger for that, and it keeps them going on days when they seem to be running on empty. If you've been surprised even once by what you thought or what you saw while writing these past forty days, then maybe you know what I mean.

Yes, writing is work, but it doesn't have to be painful. The pain comes mostly from having standards that are too high, too soon in the writing process. Pole vaulters do not begin at seventeen feet. They work their way up to it, out of sight of the watching crowd. For writers, a journal can provide that kind of practice. If your journal is becoming a place to write without worrying about who you're writing for, a place to fall on your head without embarrassment, then it may truly become useful. You may find, as I have, that it is unsettling to lose track of your journal for even a few hours. You are less afraid someone else will read it than that you might need it to think in, and to store the puzzling fragments of the day.

I brought my journal to St. John, and every day in the late afternoon I opened it and wrote furiously for forty-five minutes while Karen sat quietly next to me, reading or watching the bananaquits eat sugar she scattered in front of our tent. On the second day, I looked up from my journal and found Karen watching me, smiling.

"What?" I asked.

"You're a different writer than you were before," she said. "Now when you sit down to write, you write, instead of staring off into space. And you don't complain so much about it anymore."

At that moment she helped me to see how far I'd come. When students ask me what is the most important thing I've learned about writing, I tell them it was learning to write badly. It shocks them to hear a writing teacher say that, most of whom they see as Grammar Police in disguise. Of course, I don't try to write badly, but through fast writing I've learned to allow myself to. I get work done that way, some of which I can later shape into something worth sharing. If nothing else, it is nice to have an alternative to staring off into space, waiting for inspiration's arrival.

If you've found it easier to write fast, even if it means writing badly, then maybe you've become a different writer, too. You have freed the child within, and brought that sense of wonder and possibility to the page. And if, later, you begin to see patterns and questions that make sense out of the unruly excesses of imagination that child shares, then you bring your other self—the internal critic—to your work. As we've said, you need both, even when they seem determined not to get along.

I know it's not easy. I come to the end of this book slowly, sentence by sentence. My journal sits open on the desk beside me as I type. The soft whir of the computer fills in the long pauses, impatiently waiting. The journal urges me to pick up the pen to play, to try freewriting my way to what I want to say. The computer whispers, "Compose, compose." But I am not unhappy. I will not leave my office to find someone to complain to. I will not quit. I will keep writing, knowing if I do, the words will come to tell me what I want to know.

BB

Follow Through

Here are ten welcome signs that I've learned to embrace as a measure of my progress. If you worked much with this book, most will seem familiar. See how many apply to you, and your writing ways.

A Writer's Ten Welcome Signs

1) You are able to write regularly, even when you're not in the mood.

2) If you want to, you can write fast without stopping. You can write until your hand hurts.

3) Your "bad" writing doesn't bother you. You know that bad writing often leads to good writing.

4) When you write, you first concentrate on what you want to say, not who might want to read it. Meaning comes before audience.

5) You frequently write about things that confuse you. You learn to like confusion, to seek it out.

6) More and more, you are surprised by what the writing is telling you.

7) You rarely think about style, except to admire in other writers.

8) In revision, you find yourself throwing good stuff away.

9) You notice things other people miss. You remember them. You write them down.

10) You are able to recognize your good writing. It makes you happy to have written it.

Index

General Writing Books

Beginnings, Middles and Ends, by Nancy Kress $13.95
Dare to Be a Great Writer, by Leonard Bishop (paper) $14.95
Freeing Your Creativity, by Marshall Cook $17.95
Getting the Words Right: How to Rewrite, Edit and Revise, by Theodore A. Rees Cheney (paper) $12.95
How to Write Fast While Writing Well, by David Fryxell $17.95
Shift Your Writing Career into High Gear, by Gene Perret $16.95
The 30-Minute Writer: How to Write and Sell Short Pieces, by Connie Emerson $17.95
The 28 Biggest Writing Blunders, by William Noble $12.95
The Writer's Digest Guide to Manuscript Formats, by Buchman & Groves $18.95
The Writer's Essential Desk Reference, edited by Glenda Neff $19.95
Write Tight: How to Keep Your Prose Sharp, Focused and Concise, by William Brohaugh $16.95

Nonfiction Writing

How to Write Irresistible Query Letters, by Lisa Collier Cool (paper) $10.95
The Writer's Complete Guide to Conducting Interviews, by Michael Schumacher $14.95
Writing Articles From the Heart: How to Write & Sell Your Life Experiences, by Marjorie Holmes $16.95

Fiction Writing

The Art & Craft of Novel Writing, by Oakley Hall $17.95
Characters & Viewpoint, by Orson Scott Card $13.95
The Complete Guide to Writing Fiction, by Barnaby Conrad $18.95
Dialogue, by Lewis Turco $13.95
Get That Novel Started! (And Keep Going 'Til You Finish), by Donna Levin $17.95
Manuscript Submission, by Scott Edelstein $13.95
Mastering Fiction Writing, by Kit Reed $18.95
Plot, by Ansen Dibell $13.95
Practical Tips for Writing Popular Fiction, by Robyn Carr $17.95
Scene and Structure by Jack Bickham $14.95
Theme & Strategy, by Ronald B. Tobias $13.95
The 38 Most Common Fiction Writing Mistakes, by Jack M. Bickham $12.95

Special Interest Writing Books

Armed & Dangerous: A Writer's Guide to Weapons, by Michael Newton (paper) $14.95
Cause of Death: A Writer's Guide to Death, Murder & Forensic Medicine, by Keith D. Wilson, M.D. $15.95
Deadly Doses: A Writer's Guide to Poisons, by Serita Deborah Stevens with Anne Klarner (paper) $16.95
Hillary Waugh's Guide to Mysteries & Mystery Writing, by Hillary Waugh $19.95
How to Write Mysteries, by Shannon OCork $13.95
How to Write Romances, by Phyllis Taylor Pianka $15.95
How to Write Science Fiction & Fantasy, by Orson Scott Card $13.95
Scene of the Crime: A Writer's Guide to Crime-Scene Investigation, by Anne Wingate, Ph.D. $15.95
The Writer's Guide to Conquering the Magazine Market, by Connie Emerson $17.95
The Writer's Guide to Everyday Life in the 1800s, by Marc McCutcheon $18.95
Writing Mysteries: A Handbook by the Mystery Writers of America, Edited by Sue Grafton, $18.95

The Writing Business

A Beginner's Guide to Getting Published, edited by Kirk Polking (paper) $11.95
The Complete Guide to Self-Publishing, by Tom & Marilyn Ross (paper) $18.95
How You Can Make $25,000 a Year Writing, by Nancy Edmonds Hanson (paper) $14.95
This Business of Writing, by Gregg Levoy $19.95